PLASTICITY AT THE DUSK OF WRITING

Insurrections: Critical Studies in Religion, Politics, and Culture
Slavoj Žižek, Clayton Crockett, Creston Davis, Jeffrey W. Robbins, editors

The intersection of religion, politics, and culture is one of the most discussed areas in theory today. It also has the deepest and most wide-ranging impact on the world. Insurrections: Critical Studies in Religion, Politics, and Culture will bring the tools of philosophy and critical theory to the political implications of the religious turn. The series will address a range of religious traditions and political viewpoints in the United States, Europe, and other parts of the world. Without advocating any specific religious or theological stance, the series aims nonetheless to be faithful to the radical emancipatory potential of religion.

After the Death of God, John D. Caputo and Gianni Vattimo, edited by Jeffrey W. Robbins

Nietzsche and Levinas: "After the Death of a Certain God," edited by Bettina Bergo and Jill Stauffer

The Politics of Postsecular Religion: Mourning Secular Futures, Ananda Abeysekara

Wondrous Strange: The Closure of Metaphysics and the Opening of Awe, Mary-Jane Rubenstein

Religion and the Specter of the West: Sikhism, India, Postcoloniality, and the Politics of Translation, Arvind Mandair

PLASTICITY AT THE DUSK OF WRITING

Dialectic, Destruction, Deconstruction

CATHERINE MALABOU

TRANSLATED WITH AN INTRODUCTION BY Carolyn Shread
WITH A NEW AFTERWORD BY THE AUTHOR
FOREWORD BY Clayton Crockett

COLUMBIA UNIVERSITY PRESS / NEW YORK

Columbia University Press

Publishers Since 1893

New York   Chichester, West Sussex

La Plasticité au soir de l'écriture: Dialectique, destruction, déconstruction copyright © 2005 Éditions Léo Scheer

Copyright © 2010 Columbia University Press

All rights reserved

Library of Congress Cataloging-in-Publication Data

Malabou, Catherine.

[Plasticité au soir de l'ecriture. English]

Plasticity at the dusk of writing: dialectic, destruction, deconstruction / Catherine Malabou; translated with an introduction by Carolyn Shread; with a new afterword by the author; foreword by Clayton Crockett.

p. cm. — (Insurrections: critical studies in religion, politics, and culture)

Includes bibliographical references.

ISBN 978-0-231-14524-4 (cloth)

1. Dialectic. 2. Derrida, Jacques. 3. Hegel, Georg Wilhelm Friedrich, 1770–1831. 4. Heidegger, Martin, 1889–1976. 5. Philosophy, French—20th century. I. Title. II. Series.

B809.7.M2313 2010

194—dc22

2009014162

Contents

Foreword   xi
Clayton Crockett

Translator's Introduction   xxvii
Carolyn Shread

PLASTICITY AT THE DUSK OF WRITING   1

AFTERWORD   65
OF THE IMPOSSIBILITY OF FLEEING—PLASTICITY

Notes   83

Foreword
Clayton Crockett

IMBRICATIONS: MALABOU'S OEUVRE

Plasticity at the Dusk of Writing is at once an intellectual autobiography, a highly condensed summa, and an explosive manifesto from one of the most important contemporary philosophers at the height of her intellectual powers. Its brevity belies its significance. Based upon previous books on Hegel, Heidegger, and Derrida, it is also marked, although less explicitly, by her most recent publication in French, *Les nouveaux blessés* [The New (or Newly) Wounded], which is a reading of Freud from the standpoint of contemporary neurology. Combined with her book *What Should We Do with Our Brain?*, these works establish Catherine Malabou as an incredibly significant thinker in the wake of French poststructuralism, with the concept of plasticity being her original, signature idea.

Malabou is noted as a student of Jacques Derrida, and her thesis on Hegel, published as *The Future of Hegel: Plasticity, Temporality, and Dialectic*, forced Derrida to reevaluate his own reading and critique of Hegel in a foreword to this book. Malabou takes her notion of plasticity from Hegel's description of the subject as plastic in the *Phenomenology of Spirit*, and she develops a plastic reading of the Hegelian dialectic that involves the stretching and folding of forms of temporality and subjectivity rather than the stereotypical supercessionism that is criticized by postmodern theorists wary of its totalizing operation. According to Malabou, it is Hegel who fully and successfully formulates the modern nature of human subjectivity, and he does this by modeling it upon divine subjectivity. For Hegel, the process of representation (*Vorstellung*) "seals into one the divine *kenosis* and the *kenosis* of the transcendental subject."[1]

Hegel helps fashion an understanding of modern subjectivity by reading human subjectivity in the same way that he reads divine subjectivity, as kenotic and self-othering. Hegel reads the Christian Trinity in an unorthodox way, according to which each persona consists of a progressive alienation that is not the manifestation of a lack but "the appearance of a new ontological guise of time."[2] As Malabou explains, divine alienation is a manifestation of temporalization, a linear becoming of an event, the Incarnation, in which "God envisages himself as a moment," a necessary moment, but also one that must pass.[3] Hegel's speculative reading of Christianity writes plasticity into the heart of the human subject: his kenotic alienation is the same as God's; he sees himself as a moment of time in which he is a part, a manifestation of temporalization that achieves the fulfillment of his essence in history even as it ends. The plasticity of temporal subjectivity *relaunches* or drives the dialectic forward and beyond itself even as it cancels itself out as it progresses. Malabou's strikingly original reading of Hegel helps establish a new, post-postmodern interpretation of Hegel, and it complements that of Slavoj Žižek in *Tarrying with the Negative, The Ticklish Subject,* and other texts.

Although a student of Derrida, Malabou is not a follower in any way, and she has not shied from critically engaging with Derrida's own work. In *Counter-Path: Traveling with Jacques Derrida,* Malabou develops an interpretation of Derrida's thought by showing how deconstruction ruins standard travelogues or ethnographical accounts of uncharted areas of thought and practice, because his work consists of "a strange and perilous adventure that consists in *arriving without deriving.*"[4] Because Derrida's thought is constantly arriving on new shores, opening up new ways of thinking, it does not derive, nor does it drift aimlessly or randomly away from a fixed reference point. Arriving rather than drifting would be the aim of deconstruction. Derivation would be derived from an origin, which Derrida's work consistently calls into question. At the same time, Malabou pushes Derrida's philosophy, raising provocative questions at the conclusion about whether or not he has fully divorced arriving from deriving: "You mean that derivational drift, even if reversed, even if traversed, even if fallen into catastrophe, does not appear to travel as far as one might think in Derrida's thinking?"[5] Malabou's essay is interrupted and interspersed with letters and postcards from Derrida, and photographs of him appear through the book.

From Hegel and Derrida, Malabou turns to a powerful engagement with Heidegger in *Le Change Heidegger*, published in 2004 in French and not yet translated into English. In this book, Malabou argues that change or transformation lies at the heart of Heidegger's philosophy and underlies his ontological difference. Being itself is a power of metamorphosis, which is the ability to change form and generate new forms in a manner that is consistent with plasticity. Above all, plasticity concerns form, a mutability of and in form rather than a limit of form or an alternative to form, and Malabou reads plasticity into and against her three major influences: Hegel, Heidegger, and Derrida. As Malabou explains in note 13 of *Plasticity at the Dusk of Writing* and also in *What Should We Do with Our Brain?*, plasticity's etymology is Greek, *plassein*, which means "to model" or "to mold," and it traditionally means the capacity to receive form as well as the ability to give form to something. In addition—and this is what provides plasticity with its unique significance in Malabou's thought—plasticity can mean the power to annihilate form, as in plastic explosives.[6] The key is that this power to annihilate form is a power of form itself, an autoplasticity, because this is what allows for the possibility of change and transformation. That is, form is not just a raw material substance that must be worked, reworked, and if necessary destroyed by something else, a transcendent force; form itself gives itself the ability to shape, receive, and blow up forms. And this plasticity is the history of philosophy, and all great philosophers are masters of plasticity.

Plasticity does not function solely within the realm of the history of philosophy. In *What Should We Do with Our Brain?* Malabou engages contemporary cutting-edge neurology and draws out the significance of neuroplasticity. "Our brain is plastic, and we do not know it," but this neuroplasticity makes us who we are and gives us the ability to make ourselves and our history.[7] If we emphasize the passive receptivity of form too much, we mistake plasticity for flexibility or complete malleability, which accords with contemporary hypercapitalism and its need for malleable and passive subjects to conform to hierarchical organization. On the other hand, the image of the brain that is emerging is not hierarchical, and plasticity is as much a resistance to change as it is an openness to it. At the conclusion of her short, powerful book, Malabou argues for an "alterglobalism" that is possible if we heed the incredible plasticity revealed by our brains. Without a sufficient theorization of the brain and cognitive sciences, the positivism of "neuroscientific discourse in general exposes itself to ideological risk and offers nothing new to mankind," but understood in its revolutionary significance, "plasticity, far from producing a mirror image of the world, is the form of another possible world. To produce a consciousness of the brain thus demands that we defend a biological alterglobalism."[8] Here are the political stakes of plasticity, including neuroplasticity, and Malabou draws together discourses that are usually kept apart: the Continental philosophy of Hegel, Heidegger, and Derrida and the neuroscientific discourse of the brain.

What Should We Do with Our Brain? was published in French in 2004, the same year as *Le Change Heidegger*, and *Plasticity at the Dusk of Writing* followed in 2005. This book serves to sum up her work up to this point, and even though the neurological aspects of her work are less emphatic, they emerge at the conclusion. *Plasticity at the Dusk of Writing*, therefore, is an entry point for engaging and assessing Malabou's philosophy, even though serious readers will then have to turn to other texts to follow her elaborated readings of Hegel, Heidegger, Derrida, and the brain sciences.

Following the publication of *Plasticity at the Dusk of Writing*, in 2007 Malabou published her reading of Freud in *Les Nouveaux Blessés*. *Les Nouveaux Blessés* is important for many reasons, but primarily for the distinction Malabou makes between the psychoanalytic notion of sexuality and the neurological idea of *cerebralité*, that is, that the understanding of how the brain works changes how we conceive of an event. The cerebral event (*Ereignis*) radically transforms subjectivity, while the sexual event (*Erlebnis*) is always assimilated into or appropriated by the subject.[9] In *Les Nouveaux Blessés*, Malabou emphasizes the destructive plasticity represented by brain wounds, whether they are caused by traumas such as post–traumatic stress disorder or diseases such as

Alzheimer's. This destructive ability of brain wounds to profoundly and irrevocably alter the self makes it entirely different from Freudian psychoanalysis, which always incorporates external events into internal, psychic, and sexual processes, whether conscious or unconscious. Neurological discoveries expose the contingency and fragility of identity, which Malabou then draws upon to show how these processes change how we have to think about Freud.

In order to fashion her original interpretation, Malabou draws upon the most current neurological research and contemporary psychoanalytic works and applies them to a penetrating reading of Freud's primary texts. She claims that Freud ultimately fails to get beyond the pleasure principle, despite his later intentions, because he always reduces events to internal sexual causes, and he cannot truly envision the possibility of external chance or accidental events. The psychic or sexual event is the appropriation of any event whatsoever into the psyche, and this linkage forms a totality in Freud's thought. On the other hand, Freud cannot conceive of a cerebral event, one that comes from outside and cannot be mentally connected or assimilated into a subject's psychic processes. What is interesting and ironic here is the fact that the brain is seen as "internal" in bodily terms, but its wounding or alteration is inassimilable into psychic relationships. Brain wounds so radically alter personality that someone can become someone else, and this is a loss so total that it precludes mourning, except by others.

At the end of the book, Malabou rewrites the Freudian death drive in cerebral or neurological terms. The death drive is beyond love and hate, sadism and masochism, because it is associated with the cerebral event, the destructive annihilation of personality by means of a wounding trauma. The death drive is the augur of a new materialism, a materialism that is completely outside the psychic subject, and the subject is exposed to a vulnerability that she cannot control or assimilate. This materialism refuses the conventional opposition between brain and thought as well as the distinction between the brain and the unconscious. A new materialism is based upon a new philosophy of spirit (*esprit*) that is plastic because it articulates a cerebral event, *cérébralité*, based upon the formation and deformation of neuronal connections.[10] Although her reading is a critical reading, Malabou does not simply dismiss Freud's work and significance or claim that neurological research makes it obsolete in a straightforward scientific or positivistic way. By rewriting the death drive from the standpoint of the cerebral event, she forces readers to confront and engage with Freud and post-Freudian, including Lacanian, psychoanalytic thought in a different and important manner.

Therefore, *Plasticity at the Dusk of Writing* encapsulates readings of Hegel, Heidegger, and Derrida in order to develop a metaphilosophical perspective from which to engage a plastic reading of Freud. Plasticity does not presuppose a static structure but generates structure as a result. Plasticity replaces Derridean writing as a motor scheme by which to think and do philosophy.

At the same time, at the climax of the book Malabou stages a confrontation with Levinas by way of distinguishing her thought from that of Derrida and Derrida's interpretation of Heidegger. This conflict is a conflict between trace and form. Malabou argues against Levinas's insistence upon the inconvertibility of trace and form, resisting the Levinasian and Derridean understanding of the trace as a mark of ethical transcendence. Here a number of interpreters have argued for and against the assimilation of Derrida to Levinas.[11] The philosophical, ethical, political, and religious implications of the trace's resistance to form sustain much of the English-language discussions of the significance of Derrida's work. Malabou strikes at the heart of this issue, insisting that there is no trace apart from form and affirming an "*essentially material* plasticity."

IMPLICATIONS: THE DECONSTRUCTION OF CHRISTIANITY

Does Malabou's essentially materialist plasticity represent a nihilistic and/or atheistic repudiation of the religious, ethical, and political discourses derived from Levinas and Derrida?[12] In part, yes. Malabou offers a sharp critique of the trace as the trace of a transcendence that harbors any political, ethical, and/or religious messianism. On the other hand, I argue that her work remains extremely significant for religion, ethics, and politics despite her rejection of messianism. Malabou will address some of these issues in her afterword, but in the second half of this foreword I would like to reflect upon this issue by reading her work in connection with Jean-Luc Nancy and his idea of the deconstruction of Christianity. In his book, *Dis-Enclosure: The Deconstruction of Christianity*, Nancy articulates an understanding of deconstruction and religion that can be seen as more conventionally messianic and subject to critique, on the one hand, and as more plastic and compatible with Malabou's plasticity, on the other.

One way to read some of the last writings of Derrida as well as some of the most recent work of Nancy, including *Dis-Enclosure* and *Noli Me Tangere*, is to understand the end of deconstruction as the deconstruction of Christianity. That is, after deconstructing Western metaphysics and ontotheology, one sees that the most pervasive, profound, and problematic spirit of what we call the West is named Christianity, and the need for its deconstruction coincides with what has been called "the return of religion" in contemporary society and thought.

An effect of what has been called postmodernism has been to undermine the singularity of the Enlightenment, the decisive break between European modernity and every other form of human culture. If the uniqueness of modernity is called into question, then there may exist as many continuities as discontinuities between European modernity and what preceded it. Theorists such as Marcel Gauchet have articulated a trajectory that began in ancient Greece and/or ancient Israel, and it is this trajectory that is unique, not the specific Enlightenment articulation of it.[13] This trajectory can be understood in a more conventionally modern form as progressive, in a more philosophically sophisticated way as dialectical, or sometimes, in a more authentically postmodern version, following Walter Benjamin, as messianic.

In *Specters of Marx*, Derrida argues for a messianic spirit of Marxism. According to Derrida, the "formal structure of promise . . . remains irreducible to any deconstruction."[14] Any emancipatory promise carries along with it a kind of messianic eschatology. This messianic is formal or structural, and constitutes a "messianic without messianism" that is at work in the idea of justice or the idea of democracy.[15]

On the one hand, there are the historical, determinate messianisms, the so-called Abrahamic religions, and on the other there is this indeterminate promise that also characterizes Marxism as well as any thinking of promise, of hope, of democracy, or of justice. "The messianic appeal belongs properly to a universal structure" that exceeds even the horizon of the biblical religions themselves.[16] For Derrida, this "messianic without messianism" opens the religions of the Book up beyond themselves and any conceivable recovery. At the same time, however, this universal messianic structure can be read as providing a sense of the West, an opening beyond the closure of ontotheology and metaphysics. Although Derrida provides tools to deconstruct the opposition between West and non-West, his practical focus upon Western, European thought consolidates a certain structural integrity for this tradition.

This move toward messianicity reflects at least in part a strategy to defend Eurocentrism and Western culture by linking it temporally with its history and cutting off any spatial diffusion or contamination of separate cultures. At its limit, the spirit of Christianity is identified with the spirit of the West, and even if some of its forms are criticized as dangerous, superstitious, fundamentalist, or malevolent, this spirit remains accessible to "us" in the form of time or can be reactualized at this time. And it is here that Malabou's work insists that we cannot simply possess or receive a purely formless messianicity; that any work, act, or promise must take shape or material form in order to exist; and that, furthermore, this existence extends to the promise itself, which is a plastic form of material form. That is, rather than limiting form to make room for a quasi-transcendental trace of justice, goodness, or hope, we have to think form itself in a much more subtle and supple manner.

In ethical and political terms, the West has been constructed again and again, in manifold ways, over against its others. Its main foil has often been Islamic, as Tomoko Masuzawa points out in *The Invention of World Religions*. As the discipline of world religions was constructed in the late nineteenth century, Islam was linguistically and culturally identified as Semitic, along with Judaism, in contrast to an Aryan European Greek and Asian Sanskrit.[17] For much of Christian history, Judaism functioned as an internal Other to complement Islam's status as external other, and modern anti-Semitism was an attempt to exclude Judaism from the identity of the European Christian West. This attempt failed, although not before culminating in a horrific Holocaust, and Masuzawa also describes how, in response to surging fascism and anti-Semitism, "certain liberal Protestants, Jews, and some Catholics in tow attempted to form a united spiritual front of 'Judeo-Christian' tradition."[18]

With the Allied victory in World War II, Judaism was successfully integrated into European and Western modernity, leaving Islam as the singular exception. The Eastern religions, of course, functioned to sustain the opposition, and they could serve as objects of romanticized fascination and exoticization. The cold war then provided a screen that masked this interreligious conflict, casting it as a struggle between an alliance of the religious and democratic West against a "Godless" communism. With the collapse of the Soviet Union, Islam has emerged once again as the fundamental "enemy" of the West in many religio-political contexts. Mohammed Arkoun, similarly to Masuzawa, critiques this political identity of the West and suggests that a conception of "Mediterranean space" (following Fernand Braudel) could help undo the "fundamental polarity of a substantialised Islam on one hand, and on the other (depending on the side of the divide), an 'enlightened' or Satanized West."[19]

While the European Enlightenment came to represent a break with a religious past, it also served as a cloak for Protestant Christianity to set itself apart from Judaism and Roman Catholicism. In a postsecularist context, the primary separation shifts from a temporal break between religious and secular to a more spatial break between cultures. Temporality, which in a post-Heideggerian sense is the essence of being, composes the identity of cultures in a historical sense, with Western culture privileged as always, but now the boundary between its religious and nonreligious identities is blurred. The hard, brutal form that religious identity takes today is fundamentalism; the soft, liberal form is messianism.

In messianic terms, Christianity as such is a *pharmakon*, both poison and cure. As a cure, in its originary form as expressed by St. Paul, Christianity provides the opportunity for an opening, a universality or a *déclosion*, beyond the enclosure that traps Western metaphysics in its snare. According to Nancy, the heart of the Western tradition is a Christian heart, and "the only thing that can be actual is an atheism that contemplates the reality of its Christian origins."[20] If Christianity is co-extensive with the West, and here Nancy agrees with the reading of Marcel Gauchet, then Christianity as such "is in a state of being surpassed," that is, a state of self-surpassing Christianity.[21] The deconstruction of Christianity, then, would be to bring that self-overcoming of Christianity to an end. But would this be the end of Christianity, and if so, would it also be the triumph of Christianity? Nancy reads the essence of Christianity in terms of Heidegger's notion of the Open, as "an absolute transcendental of opening" that would admit of no closure or closing.[22]

Is Christianity as such an opening, or does it provide one? Can Christianity be deconstructed, or is it deconstruction itself—and as such undeconstructible? In *On Touching—Jean-Luc Nancy*, Derrida grapples with the enormity of the task of deconstructing Christianity and cautions Nancy about its possibility:

> What Nancy announces today under the title "the Deconstruction of Christianity" will no doubt be the test of a dechristianizing of the world—no doubt as necessary and fatal as it is impossible. Almost by definition, one can only acknowledge this. Only Christianity can do this work, that is, undo it while doing it. Heidegger, too—Heidegger already—has only succeeded in failing at this. Dechristianization will be a Christian victory.[23]

That is, self-deconstruction would be an essential part of the nature of Christianity from the beginning, and therefore the deconstruction of Christianity would be, in a way, the fulfillment of Christianity and, in this sense, the triumph of Christianity.

Along with the engagement with religious topics and themes in Derrida's later work, we can ask seriously whether or not deconstruction has always been essentially a religious movement. The deconstruction of Christianity is important partly because it concerns the possibility of deconstruction itself. Deconstruction is Derrida's translation of Heidegger's term, *Destruktion*, into French. Heidegger used a Lutheran term, *destructio*, which in its original meaning carried an evangelical connotation—to destroy the outer shell in order to liberate the living kernel within.[24] Furthermore, Heidegger's early work in the 1920s, the *Phenomenology of Religious Life*, which prefigured *Being and Time*, was based upon a new understanding of Christian temporality, mainly in Saint Paul.[25]

I contend that Malabou's notion of plasticity provides important resources with which to think the deconstruction of Christianity. First of all, there is no "pure" essence of Christianity that stands outside of or apart from its appropriation in particular forms. Second, the plasticity of form itself is not inherently or exclusively Christian, although Christianity is also plastic and metamorphic. Malabou helps us think critically about some of the conservative implications of the insistence upon deconstruction's secret link with Christianity, insofar as it asserts a certain identity and primacy of the West.

In order to think the deconstruction of Christianity in a radical as opposed to a conservative or reactionary way, we need to assert an important difference between deconstruction and all forms of Heideggerian and Lutheran *Destruktion*. As Derrida avers, "a 'deconstruction of Christianity,' if it is ever possible, should therefore begin by untying itself from a Christian tradition of *destructio*."[26] If this untying or delinking is possible—and perhaps Malabou suspects that it is not—then the difference between the Lutheran and Heideggerian and the Derridean forms of deconstruction has to do with time. *Destruktion* is linked to the form of linear time paradigmatically elaborated by Hegel. For Derrida, and to a certain extent for Nancy at least at the end of *Dis-Enclosure*, on the other hand, deconstruction primarily concerns spacing, or a time conceived as spacing, that articulates "the becoming-time of space and the becoming-space of time."[27] To think of time as spacing or of the spacing of time, which is not simply a reduction of time to space, is to see where deconstruction separates itself from *Destruktion* and ultimately becomes plasticity, following Malabou. That is, the spacing of time that Derrida emphasizes over against Heidegger provides an opening to a more plastic conceptuality, despite Derrida's own antipathy to form, as Malabou notes in *Plasticity at the Dusk of Writing*. In fact, part of what troubles Derrida about form may be its spiritual, Platonic opposition to matter, whereas Malabou's insistence on the materiality of form and her call for a new materialism may help undo such a Platonic provenance of form.

Derrida's spacing of time, which in the work of Gilles Deleuze becomes a time-image, involves the multiplication or proliferation of forms of temporalization in noncoincident moments. This proliferation, this branching, this plasticity of time understood as spacing, stretches beyond the horizon of

Christianity and modern philosophy, offering new possibilities for configuring God and humanity, male and female, animality and machine. The spacing of temporality is becoming a brain, and *brain is the incarnation of time in a body.* Here we could sketch three forms of time:

(1) The first is circular time, time as eternal return. Every circle presupposes a center, around which everything rotates. The absolute center is the unmoved mover, God as that around which everything turns. In a more particular sense, the form that time takes is its receptacle, *khōra,* which is a relatively more passive configuration of form.

(2) The second form of time is the line, as discussed above. Linear time is active in that it seizes itself in consciousness as a moment but can be grasped only in its passing. Linear time is paradigmatically Christian and is given its modern expression as the form of human subjectivity by Hegel, as Malabou's *The Future of Hegel* shows.

(3) Finally, time is plasticity itself, absolute plasticity. Here is time in its explosive capacity, understood as spacing (Derrida), as time-image (Deleuze), or as dis-enclosure (Nancy). The form of plastic time is bifurcation, which leads to a fractalizing of temporalization, an unfathomable involution. Here the proliferation of multiple forms of temporality exceeds the ability of a subject to seize them as moment and construct a linear sequentiality. The ability to function as a brain depends upon the ability to set up parallel networks, loosely connected inference systems that do not run through a central processor or programmer. There is no ghost or god in the machine; the machine is not just a machine, however, but an adaptive system of such incredible complexity that it generates new forms of complexity, or additional layers of plasticity.

The plasticity of the brain is so radical that we create our brains, and making a brain is not simply a mechanical or even an organic process. We think that our brains make us, forgetting that we also make our brains and never glimpsing the possibility of becoming-brain, that is, a pure time-image, a "little bit of time in its pure state," as Deleuze says.[28] In *What Should We Do with Our Brain?*,

Malabou writes, "The plasticity of time is inscribed in the brain."[29] Brain cells are both differential and transdifferential. In terms of stem cells, these cells possess the capacity to differentiate themselves into additional cells of the same kind of tissue and the ability to develop into cells of other types of tissue. Specifically, plasticity within the brain names the ability of stem cells—neurons or glial cells—to shift or modulate between one and the other, between self-differentiation and transdifferentiation.[30] Plasticity refers to the incredible resilience of form of adult brain cells, not only infant or fetus stem cells. Furthermore, this plasticity of modulation extends beyond our solely physiological account of the brain and into the initial representation of the self, or "proto-Self," which is unconscious, and finally into the conscious self. Plasticity indicates the productive giving of cellular and mental forms, the reception of form in and on the body and mind, and ultimately the annihilation of form, the dying of neurons that is required in order to generate a self or the forgetting of experiences that is necessary in order to continue to have an identity.

The difficulty is that we can think this absolute or pure form of time in terms of messianicity (Benjamin, Levinas, Derrida) and as plasticity (Derrida, Deleuze, Malabou). Here is the confrontation, the payoff, the stakes of the confrontation over the deconstruction of Christianity. So long as time is understood as literally formless, it inevitably takes the form of the messianic, which is a pure force, even if it is thought as a weak force rather than a strong force, a messianism. Plasticity allows the necessary form to be thought as giving, taking, and destruction of form, in a branching that is creative rather than simply responsive or passive.

Where should we locate Nancy's deconstruction of Christianity in relation to this alternative? In *Dis-Enclosure*, he provides resources to think the deconstruction of Christianity both as messianic destruction, which never comes to an end so long as the West continues, and as spacing, or, more precisely, in terms of plasticity. Nancy says that the *éclosion* or "eclosure" (burgeoning or expansion) of the world gives way to a *déclosion*, "dis-enclosure" (opening up, unclosing). Eclosure is the expansion but also the enclosing of space, and he associates this fundamental expansion with Columbus and European modernity. The discovery of America represents "a world in the process of eclosing in

FOREWORD

the world, and even more, in the process, if I may say so, of eclosing the world within it and around it."³¹ We could think about this in terms of Deleuze and Guattari's language of deterritorialization and reterritorialization. Eclosure is the deterritorialization that allows for reterritorialization, or enclosure of space. But *déclosion* or dis-enclosure is an absolute deterritorialization that cannot be reterritorialized.

Déclosion is an absolute opening because it concerns "the process of spatialization itself."³² *Déclosion* thought in terms of absolute opening and absolute spacing can be read differently than a simple messianic temporality. The distinction seems to depend upon an understanding of time. So long as one thinks time in relation to its end—the end of metaphysics, the end of the West, the end of Christianity, the end of time itself—it is thoroughly messianic and inherently Christian. And furthermore, deconstruction has shown that this end never arrives; it is infinitely and indefinitely deferred, and we live off of the messianic power that forever takes time to its end.

On the other hand, if time is thought as spacing and as birthing or hatching, this is a plastic understanding of time that is, I suggest, nonmessianic. It brings nothing to an end. Messianism is fundamentally about ending, and in a sense the entire structure of Christian and Western thought is obsessed with death. For Derrida, as for any thinker responsible to the enormity of the Western tradition, whether one is trying to reform, transform, or renew it, the world wears and weighs upon a thinker. This is an enormous and extraordinary burden, and Derrida experiences the death in and of the West as mourning. I do not want to trivialize this mourning or this responsibility. At the same time, quoting from a novel by Margaret Atwood: "they think I should be filled with death, I should be in mourning. But nothing has died, everything is alive, everything is waiting to become alive."³³

What is happening now according to Nancy is that "another life, another respiration, another weight, and another humanity is in the process of emerging."³⁴ In order to think the stakes of such a transformation, we have to think the eclosure or opening up of the world more radically: "no longer an eclosure against the background of a given world, or even against that of a given creator, but the eclosure of eclosure itself and the spacing of space itself."³⁵ A general dis-enclosure of opening/closure opens up in a way that becomes plasticity as Malabou theorizes it. Nancy touches upon the destructive capacity of dis-enclosure in a way that accords with Malabou's emphasis upon the explosive character of plasticity. He writes, "dis-enclosure confers upon eclosure a character that is close to explosion, and spacing confines it to a conflagration."[36] Plasticity or dis-enclosure concerns this explosive opening that ends Christianity and the West differently than does messianicity.

A task to which a radical theological thinking that is responsive to the death of God and the absence of any pure transcendence can contribute is to help create a new brain for our species, one based upon Malabou's insight into the plasticity of material form. This is also an urgent political task, following Malabou's call for an "alterglobalism," because it insists upon the co-implication of religion and politics. A radical political theology refuses the stultifying choice of liberal versus conservative in both theological and political terms.[37] A radically materialist theology wagers upon this world, as in "the world is everything that is the case" (Wittgenstein), and works to articulate a new materialism that would be responsive to Malabou's insights.

Here theology would remain, as Bergson claims, "a machine for making gods," but these gods would be plastic gods, and the theological machine would be a brain. Derrida writes, in his essay "Faith and Knowledge," that "it is there that the possibility of religion persists: the religious bond (scrupulous, respectful, modest, reticent, inhibited) between the value of life, its absolute 'dignity,' and the theological machine, the 'machine for making gods.'"[38] Nancy's deconstruction of Christianity can be read as messianic, as an attempt to "save" the West by associating it with the radical self-surpassing of the tradition, or alternatively as plastic, as the opening of opening itself, the "eclosure of eclosure itself and the spacing of space itself."[39] Is it possible to render a decision given those alternatives, and would any such decision not be theological in the sense of an ultimate concern as understood by Tillich? Ultimate concern itself concerns metamorphosis, the change that beings can effect in terms of the conditions of their existence. Radical theology, then, concerns the possibility of choosing or, using a term of Alain Badiou's, of forcing a plastic reading of the deconstruction of Christianity.

Translator's Introduction
Carolyn Shread

TRANSLATING PLASTICITY

Typically, a translator's note might seek to take responsibility for errors, lament the losses inherent to translation, justify translational choices, or expose some of the challenges of the text. Alternatively, the translator might offer conceptual exegesis or guidance in understanding the historical or cultural context of the original text. But this is not what I have to say. Translating Catherine Malabou's *Plasticity at the Dusk of Writing*, engaging with her exposition of plasticity, has done something to translation. Rather than describing what this translation does to Malabou's text, therefore, I focus on what Malabou does to translation.

Unlike her mentor and interlocutor Jacques Derrida, who wrote extensively on translation, radically altering its grounds and techniques, Catherine Malabou has not yet addressed the question of translation directly. Nevertheless, this note explains what I hope to bring back to translation studies from my latest translation encounter—an encounter with a word that is not quite yet a concept, the grounds of a philosophical notion drawn from the French word *plasticité*, which bears at once the giving (like plastic surgery or sculpture), receiving (like clay), exploding (like a bomb, *plastiquage* in French), and regeneration (like stem cells) of form.

Drawing on Malabou's thought, we might describe the common reflexes of an enduring protocol as the elastic paradigm of translation. Essentially, the question is how far the translator stretches the text: is this a literal, word-for-word translation, is it an adaptation, a free translation, or even a deliberately abusive translation? Theorists stake out their territory and argue over what it is to be faithful to a text, an audience, or an individual style. In this elastic translation paradigm, the key structural issue is that of flexibility, and debates have raged for centuries over legitimate degrees of elasticity, the minutiae of differentiating between translation choices and their aesthetic and ethical implications for all involved. But what is the underlying assumption of elasticity? The ability to revert to the original form. There we have it: the obsession with the original, the refusal to allow translation to take place.

Malabou responds to *l'appel insistant d'un mot*,[1] the recurrent call of the word: plasticity. It was its persistence, from Hegel's philosophy to the plastic arts to the neurosciences, that obliged her to explore *ce désir d'incendie lexical*,[2] this longing for a lexical incendiary, and when she picked it up, it lit right across the many disciplines in her magnificent edited collection *Plasticité*. I too would like to see the field of translation studies illuminated by the deflagration, caught in the blaze of plasticity. To see the inflammable coat of fabled neutrality fly off to reveal the new colors of my profession as *traductrice, plasticienne textuelle*.

And why not, when the many fields of genetics, medicine, neurobiology, and psychology are all shifting their conceptual engines or, following the term Malabou uses here, "motor schema," from docile models of flexibility that speak only in terms of adaptation to explorations of the creative potential, the resistant resilience, and surprises of plasticity? Translation might then move away from its dual poles of endless quests to establish equivalence and the thinly disguised despair at the infinite slippage of deferred meaning, the understandable fear of polymorphism glimpsed in Derrida's deconstructive readings, to affirm its synaptic genius. For what if the infuriating "black box" model of translation, in which, mysteriously, something goes in and something other comes out, were reviewed in terms of the synaptic plasticity of translation, the ability of translation to interact with its time, space, and network environment by giving, receiving, resisting, regenerating form? Insisting that philosophy engage with the discoveries of neuroscience from the last twenty years, Malabou distinguishes the plastic that yields to form—even while it also resists deformation—from the malleability of elastic. By highlighting the self-determining dynamics of the plastic, she forges a path through several modes of change, from the dialectical to the deconstructive to the postdeconstructive, in order to uncover the resonances and possibilities of the plastic in our era. What then if we begin to think of translation in terms of a *completely new conception of transformation*?[3] This is what Malabou's thought implies for a field in which the practicing of transformation is the purpose and object of study.

To refigure translation as a plastic rather than a graphic art would be to follow the path Malabou points us to in the present volume in her opening evocation of articulated masks, described by Claude Lévi-Strauss as masks of masks, masks that are plural, composed of multiple faces that open out one from another. Malabou takes these transformational masks as a metaphor to describe her own philosophical engagements with Hegel, Heidegger, and Derrida in terms of articulated dislocations and split representations. As I translated her text, it struck me that the articulated mask is an equally suggestive image for the processes and products of translation, if translation is taken not as the masking of an original but rather as the dislocation of a text's form, the possibility of its plastic reformulation.

With this reformulation comes a privileging of seriality and generativity over narratives of nostalgia and deference for a lost original. We replace models of depletion with a recognition of the vital need to rehearse, expand, explore synaptic patterning—a need that is not limited to the survival and afterlife that Benjamin and Derrida petitioned for in their conception of translation as living on through translational heirs but that goes beyond the implicit death metaphor to a more generous and generative feminine understanding of the amplification that is translation.

And so I see it now more clearly: my enduring fascination with translation lies in the fact that it bears witness to the intimately human possibilities of plasticity. Just as Malabou has pointed toward the way an appreciation of plasticity might power social, economic, political, and personal transformations, I see the workings of plasticity in translation. These plastic practices already exist in translation and always have; the task at hand for translation studies is that of revising our theoretical models and discourses away from the question of elasticity and toward the liberation of plasticity. In so doing, we in translation join Malabou at the dusk of writing, ready for the light of a new flame.

PLASTICITY AT THE DUSK OF WRITING

Variations I
FOR JACQUES DERRIDA

INTRODUCTORY

This book is a portrait. It paints the portrait of the concept of plasticity. To be more precise, it outlines the shape of a history, the form of a movement during which the concept of plasticity gradually asserted itself as the style of an era.

From Hegel to Heidegger and then from Heidegger to Derrida, a grand formal adventure unfolded, a revisiting of form that now prohibits us from confusing form purely and simply with presence, for form has secretly transformed itself. Today form reveals its true colors: form is plastic.

By exhibiting this new arrival, in one sense I tell the tale of my own intellectual life, meeting the call of the new "Variations" collection at Editions Léo Scheer to trace a path, to measure a formative metamorphosis.

The shared history of that which appears with the "end of writing" is thus viewed here from the perspective of the individual history of a philosopher who, by retracing the interactions of dialectic, "destruction," and deconstruction, sheds light on her books and the routes she took.[1] The analysis fans open within the context of an overarching stride in which the global problem of the end of writing and a personal moment of mourning coincide. It recounts a change of era alongside an intimate metamorphosis: this is the conjunction that endows the concept of dusk with its particular hue and density.

PLASTICITY AT THE DUSK OF WRITING

I. LET US CONSIDER A STRANGE OBJECT

As we enter the penumbra, I invite you to consider this, my conceptual portrait, as a *transformational mask*.

Born of a dawn difficult to place, far from France, on the North American West Coast, in China, Siberia, New Zealand, perhaps too in India and Persia, an unusual artistic trend left traces in the form of masks, all of which share striking structural similarities despite the incommensurable distances between the countries, continents, and peoples who are their guardians. These masks are plural, composed of multiple faces—masks of masks, if you like. As Lévi-Strauss explains, "they opened suddenly like two shutters to reveal a second face, and sometimes a third one behind the second, each one imbued with mystery and austerity."[2] These composite creations are known as *transformational masks*.

Transformational masks never reveal the face they mask. They are ill suited to the human face and never marry the model, nor are they designed to hide it. They simply open and close onto other masks, without effecting the metamorphosis of someone or something. Their being lies essentially in the hinge that divides them in half, which is why they are sometimes called "articulated masks." Lévi-Strauss admired their "dithyrambic gift for synthesis,"[3] their ability to hold together heterogeneous elements. By showing the transformational relations that structure any face (opening and closing onto other faces) rather than disguising a face, the masks reveal the secret connection between *formal unity* and *articulation*, between the *completeness of form* and the *possibility of its dislocation*.

Entering the evening dusk, I ask that you read these pages—the story of the past they tell, the future they portend—the same way that the shutters on these masks fold out, discovering behind each panel a consistent question, a question whose consistency itself is dislocating, for it is the question of *the differentiated structure of all form* and hence the *formal or figural unity of all difference and articulation*.

In his ethnographic research, patient consideration of the enigma of transformational masks led Lévi-Strauss to the discovery that the articulation of two sides of a face, or between faces, is in fact a dividing line between two different ways of representing a single face. The articulation of the face thus refers to another invisible articulation, the articulation between what Lévi-Strauss calls the *plastic* and the *graphic components* of the mask.

The two articulated sections usually constitute two bracketed profiles of a single face. This aesthetic process is referred to as "split representation."[4] The forehead is divided into two lobes, the mouth is formed by its two opposing halves, the body appears to have been split from behind, top to bottom, and the two halves turn back onto the same plane. This dissociation is explained by the fact that the object is conceived and represented in terms of a *double aspect*. Lévi-Strauss explains that the mask manifests a union of "plastic and graphic components. These two elements are not independent; they have an ambivalent relationship, which is simultaneously one of opposition and one which is functional."[5] The plastic component of the mask designates everything that refers to the face and body to its referent; the graphic component offers ornament or decoration (painting or tattoo) on the same face or body. These two modes of representation symbolize the doubling of actor and part, individual and social character. Interestingly, when "graphic" and "plastic" are articulated in this way, they no longer amount to autonomous entities and are instead able to exchange their respective modes of signification. The masks undergo transformation precisely because "the modes of expression of the one [plastic] always transform those of the other [graphic], and vice versa."[6] Masks thus reveal the *interchangeability* or *conversion relation* between plastic and graphic, image and sign, body and inscription.

To enter this twilight, I ask that you read my books as forming a single, continuous attempt to situate the *symbolic rupture between the plastic and the graphic component of thought* for each face of the philosophical works or problems under consideration. Essentially, I seek to connect the question of the differential structure of form and, inversely, the formal structure of difference to the enigmatic relation between *figure* and *writing*. I am trying to understand, with all the consistency I can muster, the *transformational relations* between *figure and writing* and the reason why the dialogue between *form and writing* presents itself as a *structure*.

One face opens onto another; one articulation gives way to the next. This movement may continue infinitely. The secret, primitive connection that bonds *transformation and substitution, metamorphosis and replacement, contrast and functional relation* marks the impossibility for figure or form to be self-identical, to coincide purely and simply with itself. Likewise, in return, this connection marks the impossibility for this non-self-coincidence or rupture to manifest in any other way than as a figure, to give itself in any other way than as a becoming of form. My work is an attempt to unfold all the layers of this syncopated connection.

II. MY FACES

My own "transformational mask" is built of the two side-by-side profiles of Hegel and Heidegger—that is its initial aspect, the one most immediately visible. Upon opening, it reveals another face formed by two more profiles side by side: Hegel and Freud. A third face, hidden beneath the second, brings together the profiles of Heidegger and Lévi-Strauss, and a fourth confronts Hegel with Derrida. Finally, one last face-off occurs between philosophy and the neurosciences. This single and quintuple object, this many-leafed structure, is the image of my life and psyche; both are essentially split, diffracted, divided, but at the same time, they remain mysteriously and firmly articulated.

The reference to Lévi-Strauss not only expresses my work's profound debt, explicit and implicit, to structuralism; it also allows me to summon a primitive origin, one far removed from philosophy, bringing me back to a childhood fascination with anything that splits, hides itself, appears, or disappears, without ever breaking, simply *by changing shape*; it evokes my love for twinning, scissiparity, mutability. In the end, this enduring fascination has produced a multifaceted philosophical personality. This variegation begins with a very clear and simple articulation, one that has been definitive for me: the articulation of two sides or two *logical* faces, which, as I soon came to understand, correspond to two types of *negation*. These two negations—discovered through my own disobedience?—have always pulled me in two directions at once, and it is they that constitute my paradoxical identity.

As we enter the falling dusk, I ask that you consider my mask as an object composed of several aspects soldered down the middle by a difference, or even an opposition, between two types of negativity, that is, two further types of difference or opposition. The path of my thought sits at the intersection of two logics of negation—this fork is its indisputable point of departure. According to one side, negation *forms its own solution* by doubling itself: dialectical negativity. According to the other, negation differentiates itself and displaces itself without resolving anything through doubling, so that it *traces its distancing* in terms of the spacing of a pure dislocation: deconstructive negativity.

From the start, the confrontational meeting of these two logics, these two types of negativity, constituted the troubled space of my philosophical abode, constantly shored up, constantly shaken up, by the affronts with which each "no" continues to assail the other.

I have said, and I repeat again, that we are not yet done with Hegel. I smile at the thought of all those who once thought, and who still believe, that they can jump on the bandwagon of a supposedly postmetaphysical anti-Hegelianism. Clearly the dialectic has not disappeared. Rather, the fact is that dialectic, destruction, and deconstruction circulate continuously, moving in and out of one another, continuing to transform each other today just as they always have. Furthermore, and this is precisely what justifies its multiple faces, my thought is driven by precisely this type of exchange and convertibility. Indeed, *it is not always Hegel,* for example, *who assumes the dialectical position* abreast my mask. *Nor is it always Derrida who defends the differential position.* Yes, Derrida did reproach Hegel for "denouncing the being-outside-of-itself of the logos,"[7] for having developed a concept of the negative that is but a prelude to the gathering and closure of the self in presence, without gap or difference. But there are also occasions when Derrida defends, or even reclaims, an "unreserved Hegelianism" in counterpoint to Lévi-Strauss's enthusiasm for full origin. So too Heidegger might offer an unrestricted affirmation of "the entirety of the structure" of existence, its resolutely infrangible nature that resists dislocation in counterpoint to the conception of structure as pure "assembly" or pure "differentiation" specific to linguists or anthropologists.[8] From time to time, Freud counters a dialectical conception of mourning with the terrible infinity of hysteria. Last, there are times when the research of neurobiologists reinforces a particular metaphysics of presence at the very moment that they believe they are doing nothing but describing nomadic neuronal assemblies or synaptic sequences without intention.

The actors and their parts thus substitute for one another, move around, are exchanged and in this way present what I consider the decisive question, namely the issue of determining whether the space of confrontation between the two negativities is dialectical or purely a matter of juxtaposition. In other words, is the line of contest between the two concepts of negation—dialectical and differential—driven by a systematic tendency, a tendency to gather conflict into a form, or does the crack of the gap threaten the formation of form itself? Returning to the description of the mask proposed by Lévi-Strauss, here again we see clearly an agonism between form and its dislocation, between systematic unity and the explosion of the system.

This conflict or breach of unity can also be expressed in terms of a battle or tension between *temporal differentiation* and the purely *synchronic* aspect of the instances confronted. For the two sides of the mask, the two conceptions of negation competing for primacy are in fact differentiated and plural themselves. It is not just a matter of two sides but rather a *sharing of sides on both sides.* There are two forms of dislocation in each half: *splitting* to the power of two. In each half we find *temporal differentiation* at work. This is the topic at the heart of two of my books, *The Future of Hegel* and *Le Change Heidegger*. In *The Future of Hegel*, I write: "Time, as deployed in this philosophy, is neither a univocal nor a fixed concept. In fact, Hegel works (in) on two 'times' at once."[9] In *Le Change Heidegger*, I suggested that "reading Heidegger always amounts to . . . having one's sight constantly blurred by two changes. . . . Always before, always after—such is the rhythm that marks time during our visit with Heidegger."[10]

Any thinking of negativity, *dialectical or not,* always unfolds in at least two temporalities. On either side, therefore, there are not just two but several faces of time confronting one another. From *The Future of Hegel* to *Le Change Heidegger*, I constantly had to take the middle ground between different conceptions of temporality and even different temporal ecstasies or the epochs within a single epoch. I had to come to understand the following enigma: why do such differences, such scissions, such periodic diversities, far from entirely dislocating thought, instead form the *unity of our time?* Why doesn't this frangibility, this divisibility of time and different types of "no" lead to some type of *logical and historical schizophrenia*—or "schizology"?[11] I have now come to see that the concept of plasticity is well suited to describing a certain arrangement of being that I accepted from the start without, however, understanding it. Plasticity refers to *the spontaneous organization of fragments*. As we shall see, today the nervous system presents the clearest, most striking model of this type of organization. As a concept, plasticity is also endowed with a "dithyrambic gift for synthesis,"[12] enabling me to perceive the form of fragmentation and find my spot in the movement.

To explain this strange positioning and to further justify my recourse to the analogy of transformational masks, let me add that I experienced these temporal differences through a disconcerting *synchrony,* as if both types of negativity presented themselves *together,* in the unity of a type of face. From the outset, the history of philosophy appeared to me less as a single history than a cleavage between two histories, two conceptions of history and two conceptions of philosophy. Again, these conceptions arose *simultaneously,* and in fact they can no longer present themselves to anyone approaching philosophy except in this fashion. Indeed, this dyadic structure, this shuttered composition results from the sharing of *traditional* philosophy and its *"destruction."* I soon accepted without reserve that from this point on any philosophical doctrine would necessarily be worked though and fragmented by its own "destruction," which is its *paradoxical contemporary,* and that all the temporal differences at work within a single thought function a posteriori, even though originally, from the dislocating force of the metaphysics that we have not yet finished interrogating.

Even if today I am able to retrace the steps of my path, present some sort of chronology of my intellectual life, and argue in favor of plasticity, I nevertheless retain the distinct impression that everything—the telescoping of metaphysics, destruction, and deconstruction—happened all at once. As if, from dialectics to destruction and then on to deconstruction, there was no real progression but rather all three arrived together. As if philosophy and the end of philosophy took place *simultaneously.* I have never had the time to be postmodern, if you like, to enter into the *gradual* deconstituting of philosophy. "Post" means nothing to me. From the start, the ground on which I learned to walk presented itself and withdrew, gave itself and eluded me. Like an animal, I had to adapt to a milieu that was both familiar and unknown; I soon had to learn to tame the mobility and self-negation of meaning, which cause it to take off the very moment it lands. Early on, I had to get used to the form of a dislocated face, opening onto several faces and showing me the incredible contemporaneousness of philosophy, its closure, and beyond its closure.

In the end, I learned to play with temporal differences as I did with the synchrony of aspects in confrontation. *The Future of Hegel* can thus be viewed as a deconstructive reading of Heidegger (his concept of "vulgar time"), *Le Change Heidegger* may be taken as a dialectical reading of Derrida (tracing *différance* back to its metamorphic origin), and *What Should We Do with Our Brain?* may be considered a "destructive" (in the Heideggerian sense) interpretation of Freud or Derrida, since it exposes the future of the concepts of *inscription* (imprint) and *frayage* (facilitation).

III. IS PLASTICITY A PLASTIC OR A GRAPHIC ELEMENT OF PHILOSOPHY?

In the midst of these mobile confrontations, these extreme, differentially bracketed profiles of philosophy and the other thought, time and times, "no" and "no," destruction and deconstruction, there is the fratricidal hand-to-hand battle of presence and the absenting of presence, the present and its withdrawal. To my mind, the second major advantage of the concept of plasticity—discovered for the first time in the preface to Hegel's *Phenomenology of Spirit*—derives from the fact that this concept can signify both the achievement of presence and its deflagration, its emergence and its explosion.[13] It is therefore able to situate itself perfectly in the in-between of metaphysics and its other, playing to perfection the part of a concept that is some sort of mediator or smuggler.

As Hegel says, "only a philosophical exposition that rigidly excludes [*streng ausschlösse*] the usual way of relating the parts of a proposition could achieve the goal of plasticity [*diesjenige philosophische Exposition würde es erreichen plastisch zu sein*]."[14] In light of these comments, plasticity appears as a reconquering of presence, starting from the separation and juxtaposition of the proposition's *membra disjectæ*—subject-copula-predicate. The idea that subjectivity can only constitute itself by *returning* to itself, never by announcing itself in the naïve movement of a birth without history, the idea of a *reformed*, re-formed subject, seemed to me to be the fullest expressions of presence. At the same time, according to a more current meaning, anticipated in many respects by Hegel, plasticity signifies the disruption and deflagration of presence, the "explosive side of subjectivity."[15] Furthermore, the speculative proposition also proceeds from a prior dissolution of all form. Plasticity thus appeared to me from the outset as a *structure of transformation and destruction of presence and the present*.

But I did wonder whether this type of assertion was perhaps *belated*. I asked myself whether plasticity really did put a tool in my hands capable of responding to destruction or to the deconstruction of Hegelianism. Didn't plasticity, discovered in the heart of Hegelian philosophy, suffer originally from a kind of delay that was perhaps impossible to make up? A strange belatedness, both *spatial* and *temporal*?

Consider first the *spatial* delay. Heidegger asserts clearly that plasticity is a tributary that emerges from an understanding of meaning as *incorporation* and that *incorporation* itself remains attached to a conception of space defined as *sculptural space*. How could I deny the clear connection linking *plasticity* to *plastic*? But the concept of plastic space *governs the whole metaphysical tradition*. Far from limiting itself to the "aesthetic" domain, plasticity is in fact a modality of "physical-technological" space that appeared with modern times and that amounts to a purely geometric or arithmetic determination of extension. Heidegger asks:

> The space, within which the sculptured structure [*plastische Gebilde*] can be met as an object present-at-hand [*wie ein vorhandener Gegenstand*]; the space, which encloses the volume of the figure; the space, which subsists as the emptiness between volumes;—are not these three spaces in the unity of their interplay always merely derivative of one physical-technological space, even if calculative measurement cannot be applied to artistic figures?[16]

And he continues: "truth . . . is not necessarily dependent on embodiment [*nicht notwendig auf Verkörperung angewiesen ist*]."[17] The end of philosophy makes the emergence of another concept of truth possible, beginning with another understanding of space, freeing it of its enslavement to tridimensionality. From that point on, doesn't the fact that the "sculptured body [*plastischer Körper*]"[18] belongs to the metaphysical tradition condemn plasticity to be nothing but the eclipsing of this *other* nongeometric, *nonvoluminous* space, this other space that Heidegger names the "clearing-away [*das Räumen*]"? To clear away, "this means: to clear out [*roden*], to free from wilderness. Clearing-away brings forth the free, the openness."[19] A pure, ontological space, as opposed to the space of *taking body*.

Initially, the reclaiming of this spacing thought of as an opening (*Entschlossenheit*) appears to undermine plasticity, to return it solely to the figural and sculptural rectitude of meaning. Spacing introduces fissures into space, thereby apparently condemning plasticity to evacuate and definitively absent itself.

What about the *temporal delay* then? Isn't it clearly *too late* for plasticity? Hasn't absolute knowledge had its day? Isn't the Hegelian conception of presence very distant from us, far from living thought, far from thought now? Hasn't plasticity—*one more* metaphysical concept, a simple figure or sculpture of meaning—*passed away*, already destroyed, already deconstructed?

Reading *Of Grammatology* taught me that this was actually the fate of any concept. The deconstruction of presence does not arise from the presence *of an outside*, an event or an accident that belatedly affects it; rather, the aforementioned fissures are originally within it. Hence, the dislocating force of deconstruction is always localized within the architecture it deconstructs. The indissoluble synchronic relation between the plenitude of form and the possibility of its dislocation was emphasized once again. Perhaps then we might ask whether dislocation is an even more radical threat than the notion of explosion, which is also contained in the concept of plasticity. Strictly speaking, deconstruction does not explode presence; it annihilates the *concept itself* by revealing its originary crack. Derrida writes: "The movements of deconstruction do not destroy structures from the outside. They are not possible and effective, nor can they take accurate aim, except by inhabiting those structures." This means that "deconstruction does not take place after the fact, from outside. It is always already at work."[20] Given this, I admit that for a long time the belatedness of plasticity appeared to me to be structural, irremediable, an irreparable delay. Plasticity seemed to suffer definitively from a delay not in regard to something other than it but from a delay in relation to itself, an irremediable discrepancy between its metaphysical vigor and the ruins provoked by its own deconstruction.

By revealing the irreducible gap between plasticity and itself, didn't this delay also mark the nonplasticity of plasticity, an impediment that resolutely resisted the suppleness of form? As a gap—hole, slit, cut—could it really be "plastic"? Derrida does not hesitate to claim that it can: the self-deconstructive tendency at work in philosophy, this spacing and temporization that destines presence to differ irreducibly from itself, the play of noncoincidence with itself, correspond to a form of "writing," the movement of a "trace," but *not of a form*. The trace does not derive from presence; it comes before presence, it is always ahead of that which it traces, always more originary than the form that is supposed to leave a trace. It cannot be seen and is not expected to present itself. The thought of the trace radicalizes the Heideggerian concepts of spacing and "trait" (*Riss*) by pronouncing the outright impossibility of incorporating meaning—*the trace forms no body*. From the outset, then, the theorization of writing destabilized my fragile discovery of the plasticity of presence.

The dual aspect—plastic and graphic—by which Lévi-Strauss claims a transformational mask should always be seen responds less to aesthetic necessity than to an ontological motive. Indeed, the sharing of the plastic and the graphic run parallel to the sharing of presence—flesh, face, body—and that which breaches presence—traces and marks on the flesh, face, or body. The confrontation of plasticity and the trace thus made me aware of *the impossible possibility of writing presence*. I found myself confronted by the impossibility of thinking together the plastic and graphic elements of philosophy just as much as that of thinking of them without each other. If it is true that these two elements simultaneously maintain an "oppositional" and a "functional" relation, how can they really exchange determinations and transform into the other? What authorizes their mutual transformability? Under what conditions can plasticity and writing replace each other? These questions, posed from the outset, radicalized in *The Future of Hegel* and developed in *Plasticité*[21] and especially in *Le Change Heidegger,* have become increasingly complex, engaging me in the discovery of a new position in regard to the question.

IV. THE CONCEPT OF "MOTOR SCHEME"

When I wrote *Le Change Heidegger,* I returned to the question of the *plasticity of meaning* through the very thing that seemed to threaten its validity: writing.

As Derrida explained on several occasions, in the language of deconstruction "writing" must be understood in a "transformed" or "modified" sense. It should no longer be understood in terms of its "everyday" meaning, as the transcription of speech or simple "written form"; instead, it must be taken as "archewriting," that is, the *general movement of the trace,* the original breach without which speech would be impossible. Derrida declares that this new meaning "presupposes a modification of the concept of writing."[22] This "modification" is an "enlargement." In terms of this enlarged meaning, writing becomes "archewriting" and goes so far as to "comprise" speech: "I would wish rather to suggest that the alleged derivativeness of writing, however real and massive, was possible only on one condition: that the 'original,' 'natural,' etc. language had never existed, never been intact and untouched by writing, that it had itself always been a writing."[23]

Looking back retrospectively over my trajectory after completing *The Future of Hegel,* I wondered what enabled and legitimized this *displacement, modification,* or *mutation* of the meaning of writing. Wasn't it precisely the plasticity of the concept of writing? Wasn't it the particular aptitude of this concept for *deformation* and *reformation,* as well as for the *explosion* of its meaning or original *form?* Shouldn't we assume that the origin of the plasticity of meaning is itself the relation of the "enlarged" meaning to the "derived," "vulgar," or "common" meaning of any concept or word? On this basis, writing would have to be plastic to open onto its "wider" meaning, to reveal the *other* writing, masked by its "derived" or "common" meaning. The plasticity that then comes to the fore, along with the possibility of *forming meaning,* can no longer be reduced to a logic of incorporation or the meaningful sculpture of presence in space, because it is precisely that which opens space to its alterity, *causing it to slip toward its other: the gap.* At the same time, it also returns presence toward the trace and diverts graphics, in the strict sense, toward arche-writing. In the end, isn't a certain play in form always the resource lying behind "supplementarity"?

The Future of Hegel had already tested the plasticity of the concept of plasticity, because speculative Hegelian philosophy rips the concept away from its strict aesthetic ties (or sculptural ties, to be precise), definitively conferring the metaphysical dignity of an essential characteristic of subjectivity upon it. Since then, I have ceaselessly sought to interrogate this mutability. What happens when a notion allows its ontological *amplification or increment*? Let us consider notions such as *writing* in Derrida, *time* in Heidegger, and *plasticity* in Hegel. How do we understand the *enlargement, extension,* or *transformation* of a concept at a given moment in the history of thought? What justifies the sudden constitution of this sort of a concept in a *critical instance,* better yet, in *the hermeneutic motor scheme*[24] of an epoch, which makes it possible to interpret the phenomena and major events that arise within it? And how do we explain that in all great philosophical work, the essential core can pass through the narrow lens of these motor schemes or concepts that, at least initially, are usually extremely poor, ordinary, technically undetermined predicates? How do we explain that ordinarily all thought owes its characteristic marker to that which is initially nothing but a "helpline" (*Notbehelf*): writing, time, or plasticity?[25]

The semantic powers of displacement or plasticity that make a word or concept the critical and hermeneutic emissary of an epoch are thus necessarily borne by a *historical tendency*. Thus, for example, the act of conferring an enlarged meaning on writing has nothing at all to do with an arbitrary decision or "word play." All thought needs a *scheme,* that is, a *motive,* produced by a rational imagination, enabling it to force open the door to an epoch and open up exegetical perspectives suited to it. To think is always to schematize, to go from the concept to existence by bringing a transformed concept into existence. Thus, for Hegel the specific movement of the singular is that it schematizes itself: "the singular individual is, on its own terms, the transition of the category from its concept into external reality; it is the pure schema [*das reine Schema*] itself."²⁶ Endowed with an original plastic power, the concept gives and receives its own sensible figures, its own meaningful images. However, Hegel confounds this productive activity with the actual movement of *History*. History and the "helpline" come to one another's aid. One cannot do without the other. Conceptual creation is never purely transcendental. Without the historical necessity that supports it, a scheme has no future.

A motor scheme, the pure image of a thought—plasticity, time, writing—is a type of tool capable of garnering the greatest quantity of energy and information in the text of an epoch. It gathers and develops the meanings and tendencies that impregnate the culture at a given moment as *floating images*, which constitute, both vaguely and definitely, a material "atmosphere" or *Stimmung* ("humor," "affective tonality"). A motor scheme is what Hegel calls the *characteristic* (*Eigentümlichkeit*) of an epoch, its style or individual brand. As a general design if you wish, the movement of a whole is an initiating process for action or practice. For example, as I explain below, it is clear that the enlargement of the concept of writing, the passage of its narrow meaning to its modified meaning, was authorized by the initially undefined cultural suggestivity of the "model-images" of *inscription, code*, or *program*, which activated this culture.

In *Hermès I*, Michel Serres retraces the history of philosophical schematization in wide brush strokes, showing how the transcendental imagination was first thought, by Kant, as producing pure schemes that were later conceived, by Nietzsche especially, as a productive function of mythical archetypes ("Apollo, Dionysius, Ariadne, Zarathoustra, Electra, Oedipus . . .") and finally defined in the twentieth century as the power to develop structural forms: "As [the nineteenth century] gave birth to archetypes, becoming formalist, our century tried to engender structures."²⁷ In any event, these different types of scheme or hypothesis in general aim to make it possible to both see and express "the totality of a cultural content of signification."²⁸ The scheme declines historically in so many figural ways through which being and meaning are announced to themselves, as much in the purity of a thought as in the materiality of a culture.

Attempting to define the motor scheme more closely, I tested the intimate proximity unifying the imaginary and the historical, which Hegel termed effectiveness (*Wirklichkeit*). I realized that beginning with the confrontation of metaphysics and the other thought, it was impossible to hold off the confrontation of dialectic, destruction, and deconstruction any longer without showing how this confrontation requires the mediation of a pure image in order to say or show itself. I realized that writing was no longer the right image and that plasticity now presented itself as the best-suited and most eloquent motor scheme for our time. Not only was it therefore the most effective catalyst of Hegelian philosophy, as I demonstrated in *The Future of Hegel*, but it also acted as the energy sensor and rhythmic source of a new era, which is certainly no longer the era of the dialectic but perhaps too is no longer the era of destruction nor the era of deconstruction either. It is therefore in the capacity of a new *pure historical image* that plasticity, as a still uncertain, tremulous star, begins to appear at the dusk of *written form*.

V. DUSK AND EPOCH

But in the end is there even *a* dusk? Isn't the very notion of dusk a transformational mask? Dusk may be the metaphor of dialectical sublation, the famous sunset, which, at the end of the introduction to the *Elements of the Philosophy of Right,* determines the takeoff of meaning. In this sense, the expression "plasticity at the dusk of writing" might seem to suggest that plasticity is the dialectical sublation of writing as motor scheme. But dusk may just as well signal the onset of insomnia, the melancholic state into which the psyche of someone who cannot mourn the lost object descends, someone who quite literally does not *get back up*. And indeed, Freud characterizes melancholia as an interminable dusk: "The sleeplessness in melancholia testifies to the rigidity of the condition, the impossibility of effecting the general drawing-in of cathexes necessary for sleep. The complex of melancholia behaves like an open wound, drawing to itself cathetic energies . . . and emptying the ego until it is totally impoverished. It can easily prove resistant to the ego's wish to sleep."[29] At that point, the dusk of writing could be understood as the impossible end of writing, with plasticity infinitely opening the wound of an interminable mourning, a trial that cannot be overcome. Between successful and failed mourning, dusk would then mark the time of the funeral wake, the time of the lost one who keeps *returning*: "This wake, this joyous death watch ... is the double moment of a 'promotion' and of a 'death' ... a promotion in death."[30] Even when it is dead and replaced by plastic sublation, writing would nevertheless return, other and stronger this time, speculatively *promoted*.

Dusk designates not only a temporal but also a geographical configuration. Certainly Lévi-Strauss was thinking of dusk even though it was the middle of the day when he reached that dismal, almost maleficent zone known as the Doldrums in the southern Atlantic Ocean. The appearance of this zone evoked the "natural and social" decline to which the New World was destined and perhaps remains forever fated:

> The winds proper to both hemispheres dropped away; we were entering the zone where sails hang idle for weeks on end. So still is the air that one would think oneself in an enclosed space rather than in the middle of the ocean.... The ship slithers anxiously between the two surfaces, as if it had none too much time to avoid being stifled. ... The charcoal skies and louring atmosphere of the doldrums, are not only the clear indicator of the equatorial line, they also summarize the state of mind in which the Old World first came up against the new one.[31]

In the evening, the darkness of the sky shows here as a dividing line, imprinted across the earth, separating the two worlds, the darkening of a farewell without any possible tearing, the passage to the other *on the same ground*. So too perhaps the same darkened frontier, determining the destiny of two worlds in the world, lies between writing and plasticity. The impossibility of cutting while rounding the cape.

In some respects, there are too many dusks in the dusk. Certainly philosophy appears to have been exhausted by so many vesperal confrontations. It often makes you think that nothing more is happening, that the boat is becalmed, its sails hanging limp. It often seems as well that between mourning and melancholia philosophers have nothing else to do than to infinitely unfold the dialectical sublation and the return of the specter, the presence of ungraspable frontiers in a global Doldrums, the different faces of a transformational mask that reveals nothing, says no more, and does nothing but point to the silent enigma of its profiles.

Yet despite everything, weary of complaining, weary of aporia, weary too of the threat of resentment or infinite evil, I foresaw the possibility of a *hierarchy of faces*, an *accentuation* of the flattening of the mask. As I said, I glimpsed the appearance of something amounting to a new motor scheme, the accomplice of a new era, a compass perhaps capable of showing me the way between the many discourses of dusk and end, which have always been but pacts philosophers make among themselves.

Even if these discourses—mourning, melancholia, sublation, sad frontier between two worlds in one—still accompany me and will no doubt always continue to do so just as my shadow does, I believe that by following the thread of plasticity it is now possible for me to accede to *another dusk,* or at least to *another meaning of dusk:* doesn't Heidegger say that the real meaning of dusk is *metamorphosis?*[32]

VI. DIALECTIC, DESTRUCTION, DECONSTRUCTION: SINGLE AND SEVERAL

Dusk does appear to offer a generally fitting image for each part of the dialectic, destruction, deconstruction triad. Like dusk, each of the three invariably evokes sharing and separation, crisis and forgetting, past and regeneration. In their own way, dialectic, destruction, and deconstruction are all thoughts of vesperal negation, forming the intersection of the two logics with which I began my discussion. Each of them appears as a crepuscular movement of *transformative rupture.*

Hegel names the negative economy of the movement of being "dialectic," displacing and transforming the term. This *ontological extension* of dialectic is matched by the substitution of logic for metaphysics, proposed at the very beginning of *The Science of Logic.*[33] In fact, analysis of negative structure is confounded with ontology. Negativity is reflexive—negation always negates twice because it must first negate itself—consequently the whole of being can be defined as a *doubling energy* (*Verdopplung*). In *The Future of Hegel*, I showed that this ontological energy also determined the process of *temporization* at work in the System. In fact, the two negations working in the contradiction process are not *the same type*; instead, they derive from the *different times* of thought: Greek temporality and the *modern* temporality originating in Christianity.

According to Hegel, there is a first negation, an initial "no" of Greek essence, which *roots* the thing to itself and thereby determines its stay, its *ethos*, which I have also called its *habit* or *exis*—the constitutive work of presence. Then there is another "no" of Christian origin, which, by contrast, is a putting out of the self, an exteriorization or alienation (*Entäußerung*) of this same thing—the deconstituting and *sacrificial* work of presence, a sacrifice whose concept is eminently Christlike. Truly speculative temporality, in which presence returns to itself starting from its alienation, combines this dual temporality, with the two *customary* and *kenotic* directions of the Western tradition. The *transformative rupture* thus occurs in two moments. The work of *rooting* presence is therefore always also the *mourning* of presence.[34]

As §6 of *Being and Time* indicates, Heideggerian destruction (*Destruktion*) undertakes a process whereby "a loosening of the sclerotic tradition and a dissolving of the concealments produced by it is necessary." And Heidegger continues: "We understand this task as the destructuring of the traditional content of ancient ontology which is to be carried out along the *guidelines of the question of being*. This destructuring is based upon the original experiences in which the first and subsequently guiding determinations of being were gained."[35] Even if destruction does proceed from a particular thought of *negativity*, it still does not have the *negative* meaning of "shaking off" or rejecting tradition: "However, the destructuring does not wish to bury the past in nullity [*Nichtigkeit*]; it has a *positive* intent. Its negative function remains tacit and indirect."[36]

Destruction (*Destrucktion* or *Abbau*) is not the consequence of a methodological decision of the thinker but rather an internal, immanent movement of philosophical content. This movement, correctly articulated in the line of the question of being, presents itself both as an operation affecting the structure or architecture of the fundamental concepts of ontology or traditional metaphysics and as the economy that supercedes this tradition. It is on this account that "destruction" is also a "transformative rupture"—a rupture that Heidegger presents as a metamorphosis (*Verwandlung*). In *What Is Philosophy?* he states:

> We find the answer to the question "What is philosophy?" not through historical assertions about the definitions of philosophy but through conversing with that which has been handed down to us as the Being of being. This path to the answer to our question is not a break with history, no repudiation of history, but is an adoption and transformation of what has been handed down to us [*Aneignung und Verwandlung des Überlieferten*]. Such an adoption of history is what is meant by the term "destruction" [*solche Aneignung der Geschichte ist mit dem Titel "Destruktion" gemeint*].[37]

The transformative rupture occurs here through a movement of reappropriation whose own temporality is no longer "historical" but rather the result of the "metamorphosis" of historicity. And this "metamorphosis," whose own historical origin is itself unsituated, appears to introduce a new time to thought, *the alterity of time with regard to itself.*

Derrida acknowledged that he chose the word "deconstruction" to translate the Heideggerian terms *Destruktion* and *Abbau*. He explained: "when I chose this word, or when it imposed itself upon me—I think it was in *Of Grammatology*—I little thought it would be credited with such a central role.... Among other things, I wished to translate and adapt to my own ends the Heideggerian word *Destruktion* or *Abbau*."[38] Even if the term "deconstruction" has enjoyed a fate far beyond its translational function, it is still not possible to give it a definitive "definition." It is far easier to say what deconstruction *is not*. Contrary to what many believe, in France as much as in the United States, deconstruction is not a "method." Nor is it a "critique" or an "analysis" in the literal sense of decomposition:

> In spite of appearances, deconstruction is neither an *analysis* nor a *critique*....
> It is not an analysis in particular because the dismantling of a structure is not a

regression toward a *simple element,* toward an *indissoluble origin.* . . . I would say the same about *method.* Deconstruction is not a method and cannot be transformed into one. Especially if the technical and procedural significations of the words are stressed.[39]

With both destruction and deconstruction, we are confronted with a tendency that is intrinsic to metaphysics, not an autonomous, external hermeneutic intervention. In the end, this tendency may be termed either the *self-destructive* or *self-deconstructive tendency* of philosophy.

The difference between the two movements lies in the fact that the deconstructive tendency is not, as in Heidegger, enfeoffed to the supposedly philosophical origin, that is, the *question of being.* The deconstruction of philosophy as thought by Derrida assumes the destabilizing of all the apparent unity of tradition, or any type of *gathering* in general. Hence, there are two possible propositions for approaching deconstruction. First, if it does not characterize what *is,* deconstruction characterizes what *happens:* "deconstruction takes place everywhere it [*ça*] takes place, where there is something."[40] Second, deconstruction always presupposes *plus d'une langue,* as Derrida explains: "If I had to risk a single definition of deconstruction, one as brief, elliptical, and economical as a password, I would say simply and without overstatement: *plus d'une langue*—both more than a language and no more of *a* language."[41] Deconstruction *is what happens;* deconstruction speaks *plus d'une langue.* The operation of transformative rupture working through it affects the way in which tradition is structured originally by an irreducible plurality of events and idioms. It is therefore a question of breaking with unity: Greek and Christian unity in Hegel and unity of meaning in Heidegger. Derrida calls these unities *monolingualisms* and suggests they must be transformed into what they are, that is, differentiated multiplicities. In this instance, then, the negative is clearly at the service of the *disjunction* or *dislocation* of formal unity.

If, as I have suggested, the mobile configurations of dialectic, destruction, and deconstruction constantly circulate in and out of one another, if they present themselves in some ways together, in conflicting synchrony, and if at the same time even their circulation *changes scheme* and requires the preeminence of a new pure image—pure plasticity—then how can horizontality and hierarchy be thought together? How can depth be introduced to the mask without contradiction?

I soon saw that the negative could not be my *subject*. Developing the confrontation of the three economies of negativity—dialectic, destruction, deconstruction—*on its own account* would go nowhere. The introduction of *The Future of Hegel* already sought to justify the impossibility of *thematizing* this type of confrontation, the impossibility of constituting the negative as a thesis. The three logics of dialectic, destruction, and deconstruction always fit together with one another, constantly exchanging their mobility regimes and speaking one another's languages. Thus, for example, the discovery of the two times of the dialectic, the insistence on the plasticity of Hegelian subjectivity—which "sees" its accidents "coming" in terms of dual Greek and modern temporality—are actually *motivated* by the destructive and deconstructive critiques posterity addressed to Hegel. In one way, they are *the work of these critiques*. The dialectic therefore already speaks several languages, particularly Heidegger's language, as *The Future of Hegel* also shows. Finally, as we have seen, deconstruction itself assumes a certain plasticity of traditional philosophical concepts. The three conceptions of the negative cannot therefore be taken as objects without being immediately frozen or cut off from their power of metamorphosis.

At the same time, I have said that the lability of dialectic, destruction, deconstruction, which authorizes their constant exchange, requires the privilege of a particular scheme linked to the epoch. Consequently, even though I knew that I could not stay my transformational mask by imposing the rigid scheme of a key-image onto the mobility of interchangeable instances, knowing that the elements present would continue to open to one another, moving from one to the other, I felt obliged to show how the necessary historical pregnancy of a scheme was not in contradiction with this mobility but, on the contrary, was in perfect accord with it. To do this, there was only one solution: test the plasticity of the concept of plasticity even further, examining its metabolic power, its capacity to *order transformation*.

VII. WHAT CHANGES AWAIT DECONSTRUCTION?

The Future of Hegel leaves two questions (overly) open. First, the book establishes the main axes of a debate between Hegel and Heidegger, yet Heidegger remains strangely silent. His response is missing from the account. Second, the concept of plasticity plays such a great role in this book that it ultimately lacks clarity. After reading *The Future of Hegel*, it is not clear whether plasticity is a strictly Hegelian notion or whether it is a wider hermeneutic instrument, a smuggler trafficking between dialectic, destruction, and deconstruction. The plasticity of *The Future of Hegel* therefore lies in wait for its own future. If it is true that Hegelian philosophy was able to "see" certain key axes of the Heideggerian critique "coming" on account of its plasticity, then it should also have been demonstrated in counterpoint that Heidegger both opens himself *to* and guards *against* the plasticity of the dialectic.

How then should the confrontation be organized this time? In *The Future of Hegel*, I considered only very few of Heidegger's texts on Hegel: a few paragraphs in *Being and Time* and the lecture course entitled *Hegel's Phenomenology of Spirit*.[42] Should I explore other texts, or even verify each and every reference to Hegel in Heidegger's work? A close reading of volume 68 of the *Œuvres complètes* of Heidegger, entitled *Hegel*, persuaded me otherwise. The two texts in this volume—the 1938–1939 and 1941 seminars on negativity and the 1942 *Explication de l'introduction à la Phénoménologie de l'esprit* [Analysis of the introduction to *The Phenomenology of Spirit*]—say nothing that readers do not already know.[43] In fact, in the seminars on negativity we find analyses that are already presented in *Being and Time* and *What Is Metaphysics?* Furthermore, these seminars simply announce the topic of "the conversation" (*Gespräch*) with Hegel in later seminars (1956–1957) devoted to the *Science of Logic*, published in *Identity and Difference*.[44] As for the second study, the one on *The Phenomenology of Spirit*, it gives the impression of being no more than a sketch of what Heidegger later developed in *Hegel and His Concept of Experience*.[45]

Heidegger's reading strategy for Hegel *always* involves the claim that there is an irremediable split within the dialectic, in other words, a split that is *nondialectizable*. According to Heidegger, there is an insurmountable divorce in Hegel between a purely "logical" or formal negativity[46] and a "phenomenological" negativity. It is as if there were an irremediable opposition between the implacable process of sublating time, space, and transcendence and the course of the "originary finitude" or the experience of consciousness as the "veiled transcendence" of the other.[47] Heidegger's "schizological" hermeneutic therefore points to an irresolvable contradiction in Hegel, a "schize" without reprieve. This same approach is also found in the French readings of Hegel proposed by Hyppolite, Koyré, and Kojève. Clearly the Hegel of these three readers is, in many respects, a "Heideggerianized" Hegel, a figure of Heidegger speaking under a pseudonym.

I also wondered whether there was a dialogue between Hegel and Heidegger on the horizon of Heidegger's *Contributions to Philosophy (From Enowning)*,[48] although I soon gave up on the idea. In this fascinating volume, nothing new or striking is said about Hegel. The dialogue between the two philosophers must be examined in another context and another style from that of systematic contest.[49] And I repeat: the negative never could and never will be my subject. Even if, since writing *The Future of Hegel,* I have explored several modes of negativity: suffering, denegation, gap, dislocation . . . I have definitively given up on thematically developing the interaction of Hegel and Heidegger, fully aware that this confrontation could only lead me to an infinite exploration of the meanderings of a (mutual) accusation of denegation, disjunction, or schizophrenia . . . I have never wished to lose myself, caught between mourning and melancholia, in the overly rich nuances of the dusks of negativity.

The second question that remains unanswered after *The Future of Hegel* is the status of plasticity. What role does this concept play in my reading of Hegel? In the introduction, I wrote: "The plasticity of the word itself draws it to extremes, both to those concrete shapes in which form is crystallized (sculpture) and to the annihilation of all form (the bomb)."[50] Clearly this synthetic alliance between the giving and receiving of form and the powerful rupture or annihilation of all form come into play both *in* the Hegelian text and *outside* it, without this dual situation always being explicit. Of course, I am distinguishing between an "internal side" to the concept of plasticity "determined by the way it functions *within* Hegel's thought" and an "external side," which makes it possible to soften the limits of the system and engage the dialogue between Hegelian philosophy and its critical posterity.[51] But the move from one "side" to the other also assumes a semantic and critical *enlargement* of the concept, enabling it to transgress the limits of the system and hence to supercede its dialectical meaning to introduce a *nonsystematic plurilingualism* into the dialectic. In *The Future of Hegel*, beyond Hegelianism, "plasticity" thus already refers to an autonomous hermeneutic strategy that consists in *dialectizing* the relation between a text in the tradition with its destructive and deconstructive exterior, at the risk of endangering the dialectic itself and thereby also returning its urgency and vitality by provoking its *crisis*.

Already moving toward its status as a *motor scheme*, plasticity therefore asked to be reimagined and reevaluated from the perspective of its own plasticity, in other words, its capacity to transform itself, to transgress its own limits, to displace itself, to become other. This capacity lies in wait in *The Future of Hegel* and can only be identified through the furtive play of a shift of terminology, which at the time seemed unimportant to me, although it turned out to be decisive: the shift from plasticity to *metamorphosis*.

In *The Future of Hegel* there are three main uses of the word "metamorphosis": first, "plasticity is . . . the point around which all the transformations of Hegelian thought revolve, the center of its metamorphoses."[52] Second, "it is not *stasis* but *metamorphosis* that characterizes Absolute Knowledge."[53] Third, "if dialectical sublation is not a process whose terms and operation are fixed in advance, frozen, and immutable, the *Aufhebung* still needs to be shown as responding to its own law, the law that requires it to transform . . . itself. Far from enforcing a violent stoppage of the dialectical process, the advent of Absolute Knowledge will imply instead the exact opposite: its *metamorphosis*."[54] These three instances point to the as yet entirely undetermined character of the relation of plasticity to metamorphosis. Both terms appear merely as synonyms here, equally capable of referring to either an immanent movement in the dialectical process or a tendency that supercedes the process. Since at that time I only viewed this synonymy as different expressions, I did not realize that this was actually the beginning of the continuation of the dialogue between Hegel and Heidegger. I did not yet know that the time had come to test the *coherence of plasticity*.

The most serious objection Heidegger makes to the dialectic is in regard to its immobility, invariability, and inability to transform anything, despite the fact that it presents itself as a motor, work, a replacement or sublating energy. In claiming that Hegel's philosophy "is nothing less than a farewell to time on the road to spirit, which is eternal,"⁵⁵ Heidegger sought to show that the dialectic brings to fruition the metaphysical understanding of being as *immutability*.

Admittedly, in the seminars on negativity, Heidegger recalls that the dialectic is the process of "becoming other [*Anderssein*]" *par excellence*. ⁵⁶ Dialectical negativity clearly assumes the deployment of the relation between "something and its other [*Etwas und sein Anderes*]" in such a way that any "other" will show itself as "the other of the other [*das Andere als das Andere des Anderen*]."⁵⁷ In Hegel, the "no" always appears therefore as a factor of *change*, the initial *revelation of alterity to itself*, signaled as the process of dialectical sublation (*Aufhebung*). Heidegger nevertheless demonstrates that dialectical movement does not question the aforementioned immutability of being. In Hegelian philosophy, being is still defined as the immutable: "*das 'Sein' als Unwandelbarkeit.*"⁵⁸ Yet this understanding renders null the energy of negativity.

In his 1942 study of *The Phenomenology of Spirit*, Heidegger willingly accedes that the Hegelian concept of experience corresponds to the Aristotelian concept of *metabolè* or change.⁵⁹ In the study "On the Essence and Concept of Φύσις in Aristotle's Physics B, I," Heidegger translates *metabolè* with the German word *Umschlag* and declares: "All mobility is *metabolè ek tinos eis ti, Umschlag von etwas zu etwas*, the throwing of something . . . the passage by which, through the continuity of a single throw, something is brought from . . . to."⁶⁰ The *metabolè* is not change that takes place at a precise, already constituted, moment; rather, it is the actual movement of appearing, the movement that founds the ontological meaning of experience. To think of the experience of consciousness as *metabolè* implies that it is understood as a tearing away from the self, a throwing of the self that produces, rather than assumes, identity.

Nevertheless, according to Heidegger's once again "schizological" interpretation, none of this "metabolic" understanding of experience remained in

Science of Logic or in *The Phenomenology of Spirit* of the *Encyclopedia*. In these works, change is confused with the only movement of becoming within which being and nothingness articulate each other without differentiating themselves, that is, without reciprocally transforming themselves, essentially, *without throwing each other toward each other*. This is how negativity is eventually resolved in "the forgetting of differentiation [*Vergessenheit der Unterscheidung*]," because the "not" "is just as well the not of being as the not of Being." Difference remains "unilateral" on either side of the relation to the other, just like a transformational mask whose articulations are broken. The change of the other into the other of the other remains the work of "relating the self to the unconditioned self-same." Consciousness is erased in favor of a Self whose being is constituted before the change.[61] Thus being itself, constituted in advance, "without question," as "undetermined immediacy," is not originally metabolic.

In the seminars on negativity, Heidegger writes: "Since [Hegel] a transformation [*Wandlung*] has been in the works. . . . Another history of thinking is beginning [*Eine andere Geschichtlichkeit des Denkens beginnt*]."[62] It was then that it occurred to me that instead of developing this critique thematically, I could interrogate *the Heideggerian concept of change itself*. Indeed, if, according to Heidegger, the metabolic power of the dialectic is not in fact that, then it is fully legitimate to ask: what transformation concept supports the Heideggerian critique of the dialectic?

Overall, it struck me that I needed *to interrogate the very concept(s) of change underlying the destruction and deconstruction of metaphysics*.

The interrogation would enable me to introduce a gap between the faces of the masks, giving relief to the overly brutal synchronic arrangement of the confrontation between tradition and its other, a contest that struck me, as I mentioned earlier, as condemning whoever developed it to interminable melancholia or infinite denegation. By granting a new orientation to the motif of plasticity, by leading it toward its *metamorphosis*, I would be able to question destruction and deconstruction vertically, that is, *genetically*—or more specifically from the perspective of the constitution of their *metabolic power*. By adopting this approach, it would be possible to put an end to the interminable effect of the flattening of contraries caused by reciprocal exchanges.

In *The Future of Hegel*, plasticity already designates the ability of the dialectic—and beyond it all traditional philosophy—to *negotiate with its destruction*. I extended the trial of this concept, displacing it in order to see it at work this time inside destruction (*Destruktion*). I undertook to open up the site of a *historical negotiation* right *in the body of Heideggerian thought, rather than between Hegel and Heidegger*, finding traces of a dividing line *between this thought and itself* to study how the relations between philosophy and other thinking or between metaphysics and destruction are decided *within it*, how the shift or change from one to the other takes place concretely. That was when I turned my back on thematic confrontations for good. I gave up on making the negative, dialectic, destruction, time(s), or plasticity *itself* my *subjects* to focus instead on discovering the *metamorphic structure* that authorizes the shift from one era of thought and history to another. This metamorphic structure did not belong entirely to the dialectic, destruction, or deconstruction, although it articulates all three of them. I devoted myself to considering the most mobile aspect of the mask: its transformability. *This was how I eventually came to recognize and accept that my question is about transformation.*

Open to metamorphosis, including its own metamorphosis, plasticity thus experienced a widening of its meaning so that it refers not to the play of changing form in any particular aspect or any given thought but rather to the *metabolism of philosophy*, the exchanges arranged between its inside and outside, itself and its other. By engaging in the process of self-differentiation to the point where it momentarily lost its name—Heidegger hardly ever uses the term *Plaztizität*—plasticity became distanced from itself, it *spaced itself out* to form or refigure itself *elsewhere, differently*. By losing the consistency of its place of birth (Hegel's philosophy), it thus became a traveling concept, a *trace* or *graph of self*. In one sense it lost both its *substance*—its attachment to the unfolding of the subject-substance—and its *substantive value*, since again it is not a commonly used word in the Heideggerian lexicon. At the same time, its exportation, identitarian examination, and graphic desubstantialization gave it an entirely different status, opening it to the possibility of *another incorporation,* that is, *another plastic.*

VIII. "FORM" IN HEIDEGGER

Heidegger "[never] invested [the concept of plasticity] with ontological significance. Thus it is as if Hegel retrospectively has offered him an instrument indispensable to the intelligibility of his ideas."[63] Heidegger never speaks about plasticity. Nor does he ever speak about metamorphosis. And yet, plasticity inscribes the motive of metamorphosis right at the heart of the dialectic, and metamorphosis inscribes the motive of plasticity right at the heart of the thought of being. This intersection pointed the way for *Le Change Heidegger.*

Once the absolutely determining role of metamorphosis, or rather, the role that the "triad of change"—formed by three words *Wandel, Wandlung, Verwandlung,* that is, "change," "transformation," "metamorphosis"—plays in his thought became clear to me, I discovered *another Heidegger.* In the book's introduction, I explained the principal areas of application of this triad, which I soon began to refer to by its initials: *W, W, V.* These principal areas correspond to the announcement of the metamorphosis of the person in *Dasein,* the destruction of metaphysics, and the metamorphosis of thinking, the transformation of the relation to being, the transformation of the word, the metamorphosis of the gods. I also recalled the difference between the German words *Verwandlung* and *Metamorphose* by showing that even if the register of form—the literal meaning of "metamorphosis" as trans-formation—is not present in the word *Verwandlung,* the triad of change is nonetheless responsible for informing the essential question of *formation* in Heideggerian thought.

Is "form" (either *Form* or *Gestalt* in Heidegger) a strictly traditional concept, or does it have a future beyond metaphysics? Can it "cross the line" or displace itself? Can it *transform* itself? These questions, which put into play the future of plasticity, have a decisive role in the dialogue between dialectic, destruction, and deconstruction. If it really is possible to show that the concept of form is capable of engaging in an ultrametaphysical destiny, in other words, if the concept is able to metamorphosize itself—which would simultaneously implicate the philosophical future of the concept of metamorphosis itself—then it would be legitimate to imagine destruction and deconstruction as *changes of form*, examining the relation between *form* and *difference* more closely and, beyond that, to consider the link between *form* and *trace*, a link that, as we shall see, implicates the meaning of deconstruction as a whole.

How does metaphysics transform? This is the fundamental question. For Heidegger, all change turns out to be an intersection, again an articulation between a *migratory* axis and a *metamorphic* axis. Indeed, change is always both a change of trajectory and a change of form, displacement, and transformation. Both metabolic regimes are indissolubly linked. Consequently, once a form transforms, a path switch takes place, simultaneously provoking a change in the meaning of form. In return, when the path is interrupted, turns, or inflects its trace, this *volte-face*, this interruption or reversal creates a new topology and a new way of traveling. By following the principal instances of the triad *W, W, V* in the main texts, which represent the decisive stages in Heidegger's development, it is quite clear that the articulation of the migratory and metamorphic structures both the historical and historial unfolding of *metaphysics* (its "change of era" or "transformations" [*Abwandlungen*]) *and* the specific mobility of *"the other thinking."* This assumes that we imagine the passing of metaphysics to its other as the metamorphosis of a metamorphosis, the migration of a migration, the change of a change ... and it thereby also reveals the dual impossibility of a *strict continuity* and a *frank rupture* between the two.

This *moving metabolic ground* is the *secret floor* of Heideggerian thought, its *difference with itself.* Indeed, in this thought, the triad of change is never subject to thematic consideration, and the terms that compose it (*Wandel, Wandlung, Verwandlung*) keep at a respectful distance from both traditional concepts of change (*Veränderung, Änderung, Werden*: alteration, becoming) and the change of a new era: the turn (*Kehre*), leap (*Sprung*), reprieve (*Zuspiel*), or advent (*Ereignis*). The deep meaning of change—which initially must be sought elsewhere, rather than in these well-known motifs—goes right to the heart of the question of its *visibility*. Referring to comments in the *Introduction to Metaphysics* and the *Spiegel* interview, I recalled that for Heidegger change can in no way be understood as an action producing immediately visible and measurable effects in the world: "philosophy will not be able to effect an immediate transformation of the present condition of the world [*keine unmittelbare Veränderung des jetztigen Weltzustandes bewirken können*]."[64] Heidegger contrasts this type of change, traditionally understood as causal effectiveness, to the "truly creative" change of *Verwandlung*.[65] This type of upheaval begins by transforming the look that apprehends it, by simultaneously creating its own conditions of manifestation. There can be no metamorphosis and migration of the person, of the relation to being, speech, thought, or God, without a *new visibility* of these metamorphoses and migrations themselves.

The enigma of this new visibility corresponds precisely to the conceptual penumbra in which *W, W, V* constantly sit. Working both before history (metamorphosis is familiar to us in some senses as mytheme) and after it (it is indeed a question of considering the transformation that arises with the *ending of history* through metamorphosis), the *Verwandlung*—both hypo- and suprahistorical—is perhaps strictly speaking no longer a concept. And we must face the facts: transformation, metamorphosis, and the plasticity of metaphysics necessarily engage philosophy on the path toward a *radical decategorization*.

IX. THE FANTASTIC AND PHILOSOPHY IN HEGEL

The question now lies entirely in the fact that schemes may exist without categories. The original site of the issue of change in Heidegger is not that of movement, becoming, (vulgar) time, or flux but rather the *image* understood as a *scheme*.[66] Any entry into presence, birth, or growth is an originary imaging. This is the first *metabolè*. Any thing *enters change* by showing, imaging, or schematizing itself. Throughout *Le Change Heidegger*, I followed the process of this original imaging at work in metaphysics and beyond it. The original imaging is in fact the *history of presence*. Originally, presence is change because it reflects a coming into image—*phantasia*. To be present is to enter into *phantasia*, that is, into the very *mobility that shows (itself)*. Indeed, Heidegger explains that for Heraclitus "what is imagelike does not consist in what is fabricated, like a copied imitation. The Greek sense of 'image'—if we may use this word at all—is a 'coming to the fore,' *phantasia*, understood as 'coming into presence.'"[67] Thus we are approaching the very intimate relations between *presence, image, change,* and *phantasia*. Here we come upon the *fantastic intersection*. Everything that comes into presence arrives changed, substituting itself for itself. This is the original ontological phantasm. Presence originally exchanges itself in return for its modification.

The logic of the schema as it appears in Heidegger in its invisible visibility no longer concerns the possibility of a synthesis of the category and the sensible, as it did with Kant, but rather the possible synthesis *of thought and its own image*. The determinant role of the triad of change in Heideggerian thought cannot be understood without first referring to the *imagination that produces metaphysics in general*. Indeed, throughout its unfolding, which I called its *imago*, metaphysics produces this sort of specular secretion that makes the projection of thought possible.

For Heidegger, the eminently schematic act through which thought gives its views freely to itself—which he calls "the poetizing essence of reason"—eventually concludes in the history of philosophy by taking itself as object. It is part of the history of the scheme to see its own historical becoming. Once this is understood, we have reached the end of metaphysics.[68]

But ultrametaphysical thought also produces its own image. Thus the image of Heideggerian thought and its guiding scheme are constituted by the triad of change. The fact that this triad sits, as I just said, in a conceptual penumbra or semivisibility is not because it is "marginal" or constitutes who knows what unthought thought. Heidegger has no end of supposedly "unthought thoughts" that have been shown the light of day by his critical posterity. But here the penumbra is the light of an image. The space that opens between the full day of the text and the *chiaroscuro* of its metabolic floor corresponds to the difference between thought and the image of thought, which present themselves as each other. The triad of change—with all its migratory and metamorphic variations and the great wealth of its differentiated structure—*is the motor scheme of Heideggerian thought,* hidden like a casket in the recesses of the text, an inexhaustible fantasmatic resource.

Thus a motor scheme is not simply what I previously called the constitution of a privileged hermeneutic instrument as a "helpline" or as the most effective sensor of energy and meaning of an era. These are true characteristics, but the ontological and hermeneutic "enlargement" or "increase" of this kind of formula—in a word, its plasticity—are only effective and legitimate if this type of scheme is also the *image of the thought* that constitutes it as such, its specular production. The validity of a motor scheme certainly depends on its historical effectiveness, but this is only possible if the thought for which it is the proof has solidly constituted its own image. Clearly, metaphysics as presented by Heidegger amounts to a process of ontological narcissism. All thought, just like all being present, imagines itself originally. As a whole, the tradition is the process of a long self-schematization.[69] Heidegger himself only ever works within Western schemes of thought. For him, the schematism thus becomes the *relation of being to itself*, its history, the advent of its own essence.

Neither visible nor invisible, just like our metamorphoses and transformations, schemes of thought are truly imaginary and are in fact fantastic. By schematizing itself, thought exchanges with itself, and this movement thus repeats exactly the originary exchange of presence for image—fantasma.

Before further describing the meaning I attribute to the term "fantastic" in Heidegger, I should mention that the idea of a philosophical fantastic had already occurred to me in two ways. The first is the Hegelian treatment of the transcendental imagination, analyzed at length in *The Future of Hegel*. The second is the use of the term "fantastic" in Levinas's thought, for he is no doubt the only philosopher to accord a fundamental role to the term. In Levinas, the fantastic refers to nothing less than the *specific reality of ontological difference*, or, if you prefer, *the fantasmatic effect of the destruction of ontology in the real*—as it survives the night, in insomnia and the solitude of hypervigilance, between mourning and melancholia, the desire for rupture and the ceaselessness of existing.[70] I shall briefly discuss these two interpretations of the fantastic.

The Hegelian Fantastic

The Hegelian fantastic is intimately connected with the fulfillment of the end of history. For Hegel, the fulfillment of the end of history is largely *imaginary*.

In *The Future of Hegel*, I tried to show that the plasticity of *Aufhebung*, or dialectical sublation, leads it to sublate, relinquish, or abandon itself:

> Considering the last moment of absolute spirit (Philosophy), one readily notes the synonymy between the verbs *aufheben* and *befreien* ("to liberate"), as well as *ablegen* ("to discard," "to remove," "to take away"). Speculative abrogation, in no way alien to the process of the *Aufhebung*, is indeed its fulfillment. Abrogation is a *sublation of sublation* [*relève de la relève*], the result of the *Aufhebung*'s work on itself and, as such, its transformation. The movement of suppression and preservation produces this transformation at a certain moment in history, the moment of Absolute Knowledge. Speculative abrogation is the *absolute sublation*, if by "absolute" we mean a relief or sublation (*relève*) that frees from a certain type of attachment.[71]

The dialectical process of *sublating sublation* cannot be separated from the work of *productive imagination* understood in Hegel's dramatically transformed sense. By assimilating transcendental imagination to intuitive understanding, in other words, to the understanding of God himself,[72] Hegel confers the fundamental role of an original synthetic power on God, a power that no longer belongs only to the finished subject but that also characterizes the development of the Self (*Selbst*) beyond all individual subjectivity, that is, in fact the *self-schematizing of spiritual development*, the *reflexive relation of history to itself.*

There is an indissoluble bond between speculative abrogation and the definition of history as "seeing" the self "coming." Dialectical teleology can therefore be interpreted as a process of *self-appearance of the self of the Self,* that is, the production of its image. If sublation can sublate itself, it is precisely because in the end it *sees itself* and can therefore *miss* (itself).

Everything appears. And the end of history starts off with this announcement, this implacable revelation. Contrary to what is thought all too often, absolute knowledge is not the blinding and unbearable illumination of the fulfillment of history. Indeed, this light necessarily produces its double, its image, which itself sits in the conceptual penumbra where I sought out plasticity. There is a *spiritual imaginary,* which is the fantastic double of absolute knowledge.

There is a self-image of effectiveness. The fantastic is thus the speculative sublation of figuration and representation.[73] I believe that Hegel's philosophy cannot be understood without seeing the fantastic dimension of the absolute: the image of history that arises with the fulfillment of history, the image (which can no longer really be artistic or religious, or which loses its iconic power) of a *plastic* system, a supple form capable of welcoming whatever arrives, including, perhaps, the other of history.

In the vesperal penumbra where this image sits, the possibility of a *change and a regime of events that are no longer historic* may be distinguished. On completing *The Future of Hegel*, I left subjectivity at the threshold of its self-transformation, a threshold that is also the threshold of the self-transformation of history, where the reflection of an *other* effectiveness glimmers.

The philosophical fantastic therefore concerns both the early morning rising up of presence and the end of philosophy as the exhaustion of presence. Both rising up and exhaustion reflect a change of self, a metamorphosis of presence exchanging itself with its image, through movement. While one movement is initial, the other is terminal. It is an exchange that weaves together the gradual constitution of the self-image of philosophy. Today, I am certain that the real meeting point between Hegel and Heidegger sits exactly on this horizon line, this dividing line between the history of philosophy and the thought of a *nonhistorical* and *nonphilosophical* transformation of transformation, history, and philosophy. The fantastic refers both to reality and to the mode of apprehension of this line. Hegel and Heidegger agree on this point, because they meet *at the very point of the truly imaginary fulfillment of history.*

How then are we to transform ourselves now that history is over? This question, which guides all my reading of Heidegger, is actually liberated by the history of an image. The migratory and the metamorphic are entirely directed toward the description of the production and superceding of this image, a superceding that opens up new schematic possibilities. Thus, it is at the point of this question—history and the pure image of history—that Hegel and Heidegger, if you like, hold hands, and the two flaps of the mask are articulated more firmly than ever. The true confrontation between the two philosophers can only be situated at the intersection of the end of history and the arrival of this undetermined event that Heidegger terms *Ereignis* and that also reserves the visibility of its metamorphosis. To consider the effectiveness of change in Heidegger amounts to sending him back, from Hegel, the question of the end of history, to cause him to answer by destabilizing the throne of being, to a close study of the status of beings, to meditate on the fact that the change of being only occurs in the movement of change of the being itself (*"durch die Umgestaltung des Seindes in das Seiende selbst"*).[74]

But the intersection of Hegel and Heidegger is also a point of rupture. Furthermore, it is in fact the simultaneity of *suture* and *rupture* that seems to form the most solid articulation of my mask, because it is the most solid articulation of the concept of transformation. *Today* transformation depends on seeing a tipping point running straight through the heart of everything—suture and rupture—a division between a traditional modality of being and a new modality of being, between the two modalities of presence: metaphysics and ultrametaphysics. The two flaps of the transformational mask—Hegel and Heidegger—figure the dissociation between a still-traditional thought of history and a new thought of change, between metaphysics and what it is no longer metaphysics. The *split representation* of philosophy is therefore constitutive of philosophy. In *Le Change Heidegger,* the fantastic is seen less as the main thread or theme than as a way of appearing of things once metaphysics has been fulfilled and superceded. Their image is double, divided, dissociated, *dislocated*, yet *articulated.*

For Heidegger, metamorphosis and migration are concerned exactly with the crossing of this frontier that divides and articulates all things—before and after metaphysics. The crossing occurs through both continuity and contiguity, with the abruptness of a radical break. Metamorphosis and migration are also identity changes that share the same ground (maturation, slowness) as unpredictable gaps (bridge, leap, pass . . .). In Heidegger, it is impossible to give priority to the model of slow, continuous, targeted, ontogenetic metamorphosis or to the model of metamorphosis without a predefined subject, pure rupture or inaugural leap (as in Gregor Samsa's sudden metamorphosis in Kafka's short story). Both forms of metamorphosis are at work, forming the two *cineplastic* axes of the Heideggerian imaginary.[75] The thought of change obeys this double regime that characterizes the mobility that belongs to the question of being constantly and simultaneously.

This dividing line between suture and rupture—here again a conglomeration of form and its dislocation—this line that Heidegger constantly invites us to *cross* cuts through everything, articulates everything, humans, gods, the relation to being, things... Now everything *parle plus d'une langue*, everything projects a double image of the self, and this is the reason for metamorphosis and migration. *Everything has become a transformational mask,* a differential structure and an articulation between two eras, between metaphysics and ultrametaphysics. Everything bears this "nonwounding scar" that separates two ages, two versions of presence.[76] Henceforth, the "object" of philosophy could very well be this fantastic dividing line between these halves or flaps of ourselves, these articulated shutters of Being (*Sein*) and Being (*Seyn*).

The Heideggerian view of change is obviously part of an *ontological* plasticity that decides on both the clarity and suppleness of this fracture. This originary plasticity, which authorizes both metamorphoses and migrations, is so fundamental (the mutability of presence is older than presence) that there is perhaps no reason to talk of the plasticity *of* Being—as if plasticity were some kind of quality—but of saying that Being is *nothing but* its plasticity.

Consideration of the triad of change helped me recognize two essential points. First, the possibility of conferring an *ontological* meaning on plasticity allowed me to export the concept, explicitly and consciously, outside the dialectical framework—a framework that it already exceeded in *The Future of Hegel* but in too indeterminate a fashion. I can therefore posit today that plasticity is perhaps the nondialectical origin (that is, ontological) of the dialectic that Heidegger claims Hegel fails to question or render explicit. Traced back to this origin, the "no" turns out to be nothing but a "'yes' to the annihilation of being [*'Ja' zur Nichtung*]"; that is, it is in fact a "yes" to its *transformability* or *mutability*. This, then, is perhaps the solution to the problem of the *convertibility of* plasticity *beyond metaphysics*.

It was therefore highly significant and consequent to write that plasticity "appears ... as the *center of the metamorphosis* of Hegelian philosophy," as it was later revealed that, at the very heart of the system, plasticity had already inscribed the known secret of the question of being: its migratory and metamorphic structure. Plasticity could thus lose its name for a moment to become metamorphosis in Heidegger. As in *Le Change Heidegger,* it was able to abandon the heavy burden of its *etymon* for a while, without ceasing to be itself.

The second realization was that by revealing the *split representation* of all things, humans, God, and the god of the relation to Being, of Being itself in the Heideggerian text, this exportation or displacement of plasticity—which is essential in the genesis of its constitution as a motor scheme—allowed me to *develop Hegel's implicit response to Le Change Heidegger*... Aren't the cleavage and dislocation in fact proof that there is some kind of *schizology in Heidegger himself*? A conflict or dissociation that is not entirely *assumed*?

Everything is composed of two facing profiles, the traditional profile in counterpoint to the destruction of this same profile. Yet it must be said that Heidegger never recognized this ontological *split representation as such,* even though it is he who brings it to light. The conflicted nature of the fantastic can be seen at the very moment that its discovery is immediately sublimated— I do not think the term is too strong for it—in and through a kind of worshiping of the "simple." Indeed, for Heidegger "simplicity" (*Einfachheit*) is a necessary term in authentic metamorphosis. In "Hebel—Friend of the House," he states: "it is an intensification which goes toward simplicity. To intensify language toward simplicity [*die Sprache ins Einfache steigern*] means: to transform everything into the soft glow of the peacefully sounding word."[77] Writing to René Char on September 16, 1963, he confides that "the achievement of the artist's work" occurs in the "modest" and "simple," given "by the metamorphosis [*durch die Verwandlung*]" as its results.[78] Yet what can the simple mean in a thought of difference if not something like a return, a regression toward the plenitude of presence?

Hegel's answer to the discoveries of *Le Change Heidegger* could therefore be the following: the recognition of the schizological tendency of ontology enables the dialectizing of the simple, breaking its sculptural effect. Plasticity can thus put itself at the service of the dislocation of unity *with and against Heidegger* and, contrary to all expectations, it can now characterize the *(dialectically) schizoid consistence of the ultrametaphysical real.*

Once again, the articulation of Hegelian and Heideggerian thought reveals its solidity, unlike the dividing line between traditional ontology and its other, a line that is in some ways the Doldrums of philosophy, the *split representation* of metaphysics and its beyond-closure. The frontier line between two worlds. This plastic line of demarcation between Being and Being is a dynamic separation; in other words, it is porous. It reveals the *schize of the simple* just as much as *the dialectic's opening to a wider horizon than the dialectic*. Once again, graphic and plastic elements convene, and Hegel and Heidegger meet again, soldered together forever, eternally split, face to face.

X. THE FANTASTIC AND PHILOSOPHY: LEVINAS

The second source of the philosophical "fantastic" is Levinas's philosophy. Levinas diverts the category of "fantastic" from its strictly aesthetic bonds (poetic, novelistic, cinematographic . . .) by conferring a resolutely *ontological* dimension upon it. The fantastic then refers to *the appearance of ontological difference in reality* or, if you like, the appearance of the image of ontological difference in the real, *right in among things*. As we know, Levinas translates the terms of ontological difference—Being and being—as "existing" (or "existence") and "existent." The fantastic appears when a dissociation arises between existing and existent. "Existing" is thought of as a sort of floating background of presence with no ontic status, which, in one sense, affects us only through the horror it inspires:

> It is as if the existent appeared only in an existence that precedes it, as though existence were independent of the existent, and the existent that finds itself thrown there could never become master of existence. It is precisely because of this that there is desertion and abandonment. Thus dawns the idea of an existing that occurs without us, without a subject, an existing without existents.[79]

The terrifying or horrible arises when existing shows itself in this way, separated from the existent. "Let us imagine," writes Levinas:

all things, beings and persons returning to nothingness. What remains after this imaginary destruction of everything is not something, but the fact that *there is* [*il y a*]. The absence of everything returns as a presence, as the place where the bottom has dropped out of everything, an atmospheric density, a plenitude of the void, or the murmur of silence. There is, after this destruction of things and beings, the impersonal "field of forces" of existing. There is something that is neither subject nor substantive. The fact of existing imposes itself when there is no longer anything. And it is anonymous: there is neither anyone nor anything that takes this existence upon itself. It is impersonal like "it is raining" or "it is hot." Existing returns no matter with what negation one dismisses it. There is, as the irremissibility of pure existing.[80]

This "irremissibility" has a *hallucinatory* effect. The "there is" appears as the *pure* (not existent) image of being. The truly fantastic is the reverberation of this image in the existent, the heterogeneous, disparate reflection that creates this strange atmosphere, this hypervigilance, this incessant murmur. In *Existence and Existents*, Levinas writes: "nocturnal space delivers us over to being."[81] And things "get their fantastic character"[82] from the horror of darkness.

Having become strangers to one another, existing and existents paradoxically allow the community of this strangeness to appear even in flesh, matter, or fantastic image, coming into the bedroom, marrying the shapes of the furniture, becoming a carpet or a lamp. These apparitions, the "dark background of existence," usually occur *at dusk, in the twilight, after nightfall.*

These analyses of dusk and its phantasmagoria are fundamental, for they allow us to define the object of philosophy in a radically new manner: as an *imaginary object*. This imaginary "object" is Being itself, the powerfully hallucinatory effect of its phenomena.

It is only possible to tear away from the horror of the "there is" through the hooking back of *transcendence,* the act and affirmation of singular existence through which the existent is able to break with the permanent background or "hypostasis" of existing. For Levinas, the fantastic is entirely *soluble in transcendence.* The alterity of existence for the existent can always bring an end to it. By contrast, in Heidegger the fantastic is precisely the impossibility of escaping the "background" . . . *Heidegger is not a transcendent thinker;* it is essential to understand this to grasp his philosophy, which claims the existence of an *alterity without an outside.*

It is true that for Heidegger there is no "otherwise than being." Nor is there, consequently, any beyond essence. In some ways, the frontiers of Being cannot be transgressed. But this lack of beyond, which motivates change, does not imply a lack of alterity, nor does it imply "the reduction of the other to the same."[83] *Le Change Heidegger* seeks to argue against claims such as: "If transcendence has meaning, it can only signify the fact that the *event of being,* the *esse,* the *essence,* passes over to what is other than being."[84] Or: "essence cannot be thought otherwise, thought can only be beyond essence."[85] Today I have serious reservations about such a "beyond." All in all, I have never really believed in an alterity of pure dissymmetry. Perhaps it comes from some sort of dialectical stubbornness, but I can believe only in the concept of an articulated alterity, attached to that of which it is the alterity, dislocated but always bespoken or *taken,* in the same way that we say that something *takes form.*

The problem in "otherwise than being" lies in the modality of *passage* to the otherwise. What changes from "being" to "otherwise than being"? Is it a mere crossing, a migration, a metamorphosis? Levinas is silent on this point, as if his emphasis on the Other alone settles the question, as if the revelation of the fragility of the Other were enough to ensure the conversion or ethical transformation of the look and the transgression of ontology. As if there were no negotiation and no conversion to be done to leave the horrible immanence, the fantastic hypostasis. For Heidegger, on the other hand, what matters is *metamorphic and migratory mediation*—which is also a *remedy* for the absence of an outside—without which the other could never present itself. I have already said that the *movement of alterity is a cineplastic, not a revelatory aplastic or akinesia.* In Heidegger, there is no alterity outside the change that makes alterity possible, there is no other that is not, one way or another, *introduced by W, W, V.* Not simply because changing is by definition "becoming other" or "being otherwise" but mainly because alterity can only impose itself fundamentally through its *power of transformation* and as this same power. Transformation is the origin of alterity.

Let us recall Heidegger's comment in *On the Way to Language:* "To undergo an experience with something—be it a thing, a person, or a god—means that this something befalls us, strikes us, comes over us, overwhelms and transforms us [*über uns kommt, uns unwirft und verwandelt*]."[86] This metamorphosis is at once a change of route, a new direction, and a change of form. To undergo an experience is to receive another inflection and another form from the other as well as to give the other these changes in return. In *Language in the Poem,* Heidegger calls this form "essential form [*Wesensgestalt*]."[87] This form-effect of the other may be that of a thing, a person, or a god but may equally well be a new thought. Heidegger cites Nietzsche's aphorism, which says of eternal return: "If that thought ever came to prevail in you, it would metamorphosise you . . . perhaps it would mangle you."[88] Yet Levinas never mentions this relation between alterity and change, this plasticity of the other.

Once again, even if an alterity of metamorphosis and migration is not an alterity of pure dissymmetry, it is not a false alterity nor a pretext-alterity either. The other in Heidegger is not *beyond essence* but is *other in the essential.* Indeed, metamorphosis makes it possible to discover the other "in what is essential [*im Wesentlichen anders*]."[89] Heidegger distinguishes between "alterity" and "proximity" "in the essential," where proximity in the essential refers to belonging to tradition. For example, "no matter how far removed Nietzsche is from Descartes and no matter how much he emphasizes the distance [*Weit*] between them, in what is essential he still stands close to Descartes [*so nahe steht er ihm doch im Wesentlichen*]."[90] Alterity in the essential refers first to the *alterity of essence to its metaphysical meaning. It is not therefore a matter of an other from essence but rather of an other essence.* Again, no outside, but the radical alterity of ontological determinations to themselves. The other in the essential reveals first the strangeness of its essence *there where an outside is lacking.* This is the common definition of the fantastic, in which the frightening, the surprising, and the strange always arise from that which is *already there.*

Sartre states clearly that the fantastic is in some ways dependent on the possibility of seeing the inside "from the outside." An outside that is nothing but the resource of an inside or "a ghost of transcendence": "How is one to make him see *from the outside* this obligation to be inside? Such is, fundamentally, the problem posed for Blanchot and Kafka. . . . Here is the solution they have found: they have eliminated the angel's gaze and have plunged the reader into the world with K. and Thomas; but they have left, as it were, a ghost of transcendence, floating about within this immanence."[91] Certainly, there is no immanent ontological circulation in Heidegger, but the hooking back, the exit or frank irruption are also impossible in his philosophy. If the issue of change originates in the question of the image, that is because the image dictates a specific type of mobility based on the impossibility for us to escape its look. We are looked at by the look.[92]

Changing therefore amounts to finding a mode of torsion, reversion, metamorphosis, or migration that matches the impossibility of fleeing and the injunction to look at what looks at us. It is a kind of flight *in situ*, if you like, as envisaged in the third part of *Le Change Heidegger* on the topic of "modification" in *Being and Time*. To modify oneself is to change without fleeing, running, or waiting. Thus, the fantastic in Heidegger depends not only on the pregnancy of the image but also on the invention of the very specific change to which this same pregnancy condemns us—I have compared this type of change to the "peregrination" of the insect Samsa on the walls of his room. To transform oneself right here on the spot.

Originally, the essence of a thing (Heidegger calls it *Wesung*, but it could equally well be *Unwesen*) is its alterity. The essence of a thing is that through which it is originally foreign to itself. It should be possible to understand that alterity is first of all the strangeness within, the most intimate unexplored mystery of essential self-identity. Heidegger recalls that the stranger, *fremd, der Fremde*, comes from the High German *fram*, which, unlike the Latin *alius*, does not include any reference to a foreign origin, outside, or exterior in general. *Der Fremde* is the stranger who is already there and who therefore destines thought to engage in the movement of transformation to meet the stranger, a movement that is of course a setting off toward an elsewhere but which at the same time never abandons an infinite nostalgia (*Sehnsucht*) for a constant return to the country within. Being is nostalgic for its own essence.[93]

If we do not turn to look toward this other alterity, this essential alterity that slumbers in each thing in the diverting from itself to the origin, translating it at birth if you will, then we change nothing. If we do not change other, we change nothing. By following the triad of change, we notice that nothing exists that is not already changed, transformed, metamorphosized. Hence, when Heidegger announces the *Wandlung* or transformation of metaphysics, the *Verwandlung* or metamorphosis of the individual's *Dasein*, the metamorphosis of speech, change in the relation to being, the metamorphosis of Being, essence or being, the transformation of the god, he is not predicting the arrival of some kind of messianic phenomenon ready to ravish the self-equivalence of fixed and resolutely self-identical instances. Rather, he speaks of the transformation of instances that are *already transformed, already changed,* instances that are in some senses susceptible to relaunching their mutation through a secret ontological resource. There would be no other thought, no other beginning, if metaphysics, humans, god, the *logos*, Being, being, and essence were not, originally, mutants. To change, therefore, necessarily amounts to transforming transformation and understanding that alterity arises from this intrametabolic upheaval.

Alterity enchanted by disenchantment: alterity must be sought out everywhere that there is metamorphosis, in all the folds of metaphysics, as the fabulous unconscious of ontology. Everywhere that it promises another figure of being, and hence another figure of difference. In Heidegger, the long metamorphic and migratory journey is confused with the history of being and unfolds both along a continuous axis, like the insect that emerges from the chrysalis, and in that disruptive, unexpected, ateleological manner, as if change suddenly surprises and upsets its own metabolism. The fantastic is found there, in this paradoxical unity, this synthesis of continuous transformation and sudden interruption, of the reformed formation and searing explosion, the route and the *Holzweg* (the path that leads nowhere), between the emergence of form and its annihilation. Being is none other than changing forms; being is nothing but its own mutability.

We cannot leave Being. Being is that which it is impossible to escape and this destines Being itself, and everything along with it, to metamorphosis. The *condemnation to metamorphosis for lack of an outside* is therefore not only the fact of the "existent" or *Dasein* but also characterizes the question of Being as a whole, the impossibility that this question can escape itself.

And with no irruptive transcendence, there is no open door to the pure event. Nor any messianism. Nothing happens except self-transformation. From modification to metamorphosis, from migration to modification, the torsions, *volte-faces*, and reversals of a single impossibility of escaping unfold. And this background that sits right there constitutes the profound solidarity of Hegelian and Heideggerian thought: there is no outside, nor is there any immobility. The plasticity of unavoidable transformation. The lifeline of a radical transformation without exoticism. In Heidegger, the *ontological economy*, the original exchangeability of Being and being, is the metabolism of the relation to any other.

XI. THE ONTOLOGICAL ECONOMY, OR ABSOLUTE CONVERTIBILITY

Economy is the key term here. Indeed, for Heidegger, ontology is an economy. There is nothing beyond it, nothing beyond the game. Nothing but the original circulation of change, exchange, and substitution.

Western thought proceeds from an initial change—the exchange of Being for essence, understood as beingness (*Seindheit*)—which prepares its own metamorphosis and gives rise to the other change—the exchange of being for its own essence (*Anwesen*). This *absolute ontological mutability*, governed by a lack of outside, is the economic space in which Heidegger's thought unfurls. The original exchangeability of Being and being should not be seen as an abstract given, a pure metaphysical process. On the contrary, Heidegger never stops talking about value (*Wert*), "worth [*gelten*]," equivalence, poverty, gift . . . French debates on these questions have tended to erase the effective, pragmatic significance of these motifs, transforming them into who knows what "aneconomic" instances, stripped of any relation to objects. It is imperative that we resist this tendency. Indeed, in Heidegger's philosophy *metaphysics* and *capitalism* coincide: hence too, "*other thought*" and *revolution* coincide. The two logics at work in Western change are generalized equivalence (*Geltung*)—everything is equal to everything, any being can be exchanged for an other according to the mercantile arrogance of calculus—and favor (*Gunst*)—the future exchange is exchange by *disappropriation*.

Is the reign of *Geltung*, the first change, or metaphysics, anything more than a fetishizing movement of being? Can the substitution of beingness for Being be understood otherwise than it has for over twenty centuries in the West? Is this not the other name for an ontological capitalism in which calculus and inspection reign? As for the other thought, the thought of the gift as a favor: isn't this the name of a thought that is modest, small (*Gering*), an exchange *without interest*?

This is how the fantastic, as a mode of Being of the ontological metabolism, names not only the origin of ontology itself but also the origin of all exchanges: monetary exchange, exchange of values, sexual exchange, language exchange, exchanging looks.[94] The plasticity of the relation between Being and being, which is the other name for their exchangeability, the plasticity of the terms exchanged, is both a material *and* essential plasticity. It is an *essentially material* plasticity.

It should also be said that despite the still widely held belief, the emphasis on the difference between Being and being in Heidegger does not imply any "devalorization" of being. Let us not forget: the truth of Being can only arise "through the transformation of being in being itself [*durch die Umgestaltung des Seiendes in das Seiende selbst*]."[95]

I realize that in the name of ontological economy or the mutual exchangeability of Being and being, I have done nothing but think through and affirm the *mutual convertibility of trace and form* in an attempt to put an end to the *dematerialization* and *demonetarization* of contemporary philosophy.

For Levinas, the conversion of trace into form is impossible. In *Otherwise Than Being* he declares, "the trace [is] inconvertible into forms."[96] The site of disruptive transcendence, which enables the escape from its fantastic fascination, occurs as a *divorce between form and trace*. Transcendence necessarily *breaks through form*. The Other is a farewell to form, to the plastic sticking of and in hypostasis. This is echoed by the highly questionable claim that all real resistance is ideal, that resistance is never material. Indeed, according to Levinas, *form does not resist*.[97]

The Other is never the one who "appeared in plastic form as an image, a portrait," for the Other's beauty is the "supreme presence ... breaking through its plastic form with youth,"[98] for which it resists. Plasticity is still assigned to the field of sculpture, riveted to its function of incorporation or figuration in general, a delayed function, which is always older than the face. The face is precisely that which is not plastic: in contrast, it can only "pierce its own plastic image,"[99] "break up form."[100] It sits *beyond form*. It is a *pure trace*: "this existence abandoned by all and by itself, a trace of itself, imposed on *me*, assigns me in my last refuge with an incomparable force of assignation, inconvertible into forms. Forms would give me at once a countenance."[101]

Although the appearance of the face, its "epiphany," invariably provokes an upheaval—in both the other and myself—this is not the result of a *transformation* but of a *rude gap without origin*. "The face of the Other at each moment destroys and overflows the plastic image it leaves me."[102] There is no appeal against this destruction: "*The absolute experience is not disclosure but revelation: a coinciding of the expressed with him who expresses, which is the privileged manifestation of the Other, the manifestation of a face over and beyond form. Form*—incessantly betraying its own manifestation, congealing into a plastic form, for it is adequate to the same—alienates the exteriority of the other."[103] Form would therefore always be derived from the look of the trace, which explains why it is so easy to pierce it, *undo* it, *explode* it.

It strikes me as important to break with this conception of form as something that is retarded, something that must, in the true sense, remain behind. For it is increasingly clear to me that form cannot be "undone" without calling on *the support of form*, including the aid of its power of explosion. *There is no exceeding of form that does not assume the plasticity of form and hence its convertibility*. If we accept, as I have tried to show first with Hegel and then with Heidegger, that alterity can be thought without the aid of transcendence, if it is true that there is nothing outside, nothing beyond—outside the economy and outside the exchangeability or mutability of Being—then *there is no inconverti-*

bility. *Absolute convertibility, the migratory and metamorphic resource of alterity, is the rule. Absolute exchangeability is the structure.*

The trace is inconvertible into forms. Levinas's phrase can be explained as follows: the graphic element (of otherwise than Being)—namely the *trace*—definitively dissociates itself from the plastic element (of Being)—namely *form*. The graphic and the plastic are thus inconvertible to one another. We must recognize that strictly speaking neither the trace of the Other in Levinas nor writing in Derrida are metamorphic instances. Both writing and the line are irreducibly foreign to form. Metamorphosis has no deconstructive power, because form is resolutely a concept with no future. Yet *it is exactly this dissociation between the plastic and the graphic and its claim to be definitive and untransgressable that we must now reconsider.*

It is surprising to see that in his article "*Différance*" Derrida does not recognize an essential, even if banal, meaning of the word "difference," namely "change," "variation," or "variant." According to the dictionary, to be different is, among other things, to be changed, unrecognizable, modified, transformed. Differentiation can thus *also* refer to transformation. But this meaning does not appear clearly in the text. Derrida writes:

> We know that the verb *différer* ... has two meanings which seem quite distinct [Translator's note: In English, the two distinct meanings of the Latin *differre* have become two separate words: to "defer" and to "differ"]: the action of putting off until later, of taking into account, of taking account of time and of the forces of an operation that implies an economical calculation, a detour, a delay, a relay, a reserve, a representation—concepts that I would summarize here in a word I have never used but that could be inscribed in this chain: *temporization*.

Second: "to be not identical, to be other, discernable, etc."[104] The meaning of *transformation*, of *becoming other, through metamorphosis*, for example, remains in the shadows. *Différance* is never characterized as a change of form.[105]

And for good reason. According to Derrida, "form" names only the captivity of the meaning of Being "in the categories of being or beingness."[106] It is therefore tributary to the ontic register, marking its irreparable delay. In "Form and Meaning," Derrida claims that all thought of form, even that which believes it is criticizing the traditional concepts of *eidos* or *morphè,* is forever prisoner to metaphysics.

> How could it be otherwise? As soon as we utilize the concept of form—even if to criticize *an other* concept of form—we inevitably have recourse to the self-evidence of a kernel of meaning. And the medium of this self-evidence can be nothing other than the language of metaphysics. In this language we know what "form" means, how the possibility of its variations is regulated, what its limit is, and in what field all imaginable objections to it are to be maintained. The system of oppositions in which something like form, the formality of form, can be thought, is a finite system. Moreover, it does not suffice to say that "form" has a *meaning* for us, a center of self-evidence, or that its *essence* as such is given for us: in truth, this concept cannot be, and never could be, dissociated from the concept of appearing, of meaning, of self-evidence, of essence. Only a form is *self-evident,* only a form has or is an *essence,* only a form *presents itself* as such. This is an assured point, a point that no interpretation of Platonic or Aristotelian conceptuality can displace. All the concepts by means of which *eidos* or *morphè* have been translated or determined refer to the theme of *presence in general.* Form is presence itself. Formality is whatever aspect of the thing in general presents itself, lets itself be seen, gives itself to be thought.[107]

Hence for Derrida, the Heideggerian thought of a form that is irreducible to its metaphysical concept—this *Wesensgestalt* (essential figure) metamorphosized and diverted from the gods, humans, or philosophy—remains renewable as the "foyer of meaning" of presence. Unlike form, for both Derrida and Levinas, the trace "no longer belongs to the horizon of Being," "exceeds the truth of Being."[108] It therefore follows that it also exceeds the register of formation, formality, or format.[109] The exceeding of metaphysics is not, and cannot be, literally speaking, a metamorphosis.

I gradually came to take my distance from these claims through the observation that only the vocabulary of displacement and migration, the *metastatic* lexicon, without its *metamorphic* corollary, was required, by both philosophers, to speak of the *frayage* or facilitation of the trace—in other words, all that is needed is a *purely graphic* lexicon. In Levinas, the trace is more ancient than any past. In this sense, it is "the past of the Other."[110] The images privileged by this kind of *past* are always those of a *passage* in terms of displacement, scratching, crossing out, striating, all of which concord with the paradigmatic value of the *line with no form*.[111] Indeed, if the trace had an image, it would be the image of slicing or deleting, never a rhythm, never a figure, never a contour.

As for dissemination, Derrida writes that it "displaces."[112] But its displacements are not metamorphoses; rather, they are "breaks, as reinscriptions in a heterogeneous system, mutations, separations without origin."[113] The specific mobility of difference, as reinterpreted by Heidegger and those following him, is essentially reduced to the *journey*, the *transfer*, the *change of place* in general. But might it not appear that by proceeding in this way deconstruction repeats, in another time, another age, *the reduction of the metabolic to the phoronomic, a reduction that Heidegger ultimately confuses with metaphysics*? As we know, early on Heidegger discusses something along the lines of a philosophical impoverishment of movement that causes it to reduce itself to only the rectilinear trajectory, thereby cutting it off from its understanding of alteration, formation or deformation, genesis and decline. In short, from its relation to life. This impoverishment, already present in Aristotle, is completed in modern physics.[114] But without form, isn't the journey of writing also reduced to a type of phoronomy, to displacement without metamorphic adventure? In the end, isn't writing confused with its own force of inertia?

Perhaps the other makes "its entry" as a line that scratches, tears, slices, striates. But if I were not willing to receive it, if my ontological metabolism were not ready for it, I would have no reason to welcome the phenomenon. *One must be in good shape to welcome the trace*. I do not believe in the absence of form or in a possible beyond of form any more than I believe in transcendence or the absence of negativity. Form is the metamorphizable but immovable barrier of thought. *Writing will never abolish form. The trace will never pierce the figure*. A new trend in contemporary sculpture bears witness to this. One of the most striking sculptors involved is Giuseppe Penone, whose work is devoted to forming the trace, as if the trace were the raw material of an *ultrametaphysical development of the concept of form* and hence *an ultrametaphysical development of the understanding of sculpture*: "a trace formed by the images I have on hand."[115]

Discussing this new form, the conclusion to *Le Change Heidegger* develops the alternative presented in the dialogue with Jünger in *Contribution to the Question of Being*: either form can cross the line (of metaphysics) or it cannot. But if form cannot cross the line, then there is no alterity for metaphysics. In a sense, *there is no alterity at all*. I'm laying my bets for the meaning of my work on the success of the first term of this alternative. In other words, I believe in the future not of the other of form but of the *other form*, a form that no longer corresponds to its traditional concept, which, as I said in *Le Change Heidegger*, engenders the solidarity of *form-figure-idea-essence-picture*. Traditional form and the other form — the form of absolute exchangeability, or "ontological porosity"[116] — thus confront each other abreast the same mask. *There are no graphics and no tracing without metamorphosis.* I have called this *new condition of supplementarity* "change."

But I still have my doubts. Aren't these kinds of claims, again, late in regard to what they oppose? Isn't leading the trace back to a certain derivative relation with form a merely retrograde step, tying back into presence, denying its deconstruction one way or another?

I'll take the risk of saying that this is not in fact the case. I'll take the risk of claiming that *form* and *presence* do not get confused, at least *not always*, and that this *excess of form in regard to presence*—which is exactly the metamorphosis of the traditional concept of form—is perhaps the exegetic resource not only of destruction but also of the deconstruction of tradition itself. In fact, it is not possible to view destruction and deconstruction as pure ruptures, pure gaps, or pure piercings. The change that leads to the exceeding of metaphysics must be thought and this change necessarily occur through a negotiation between form and form, through a *metamorphic negotiation*. The gap, the rupture, the piercing, the mobility of the trace do not have any power to declaustrate or transgress *by* and *in themselves*. A trans-formation, in the literal sense, must take place, opening the depth of a new referentiality or another body in both the structure *and* in its dislocation.

XII. A NEW READING METHOD

It seems to me that these questions have the power to engage the dialogue between dialectic, destruction, and deconstruction anew. First of all, they open the way to a new approach toward things and texts, a new reading method. We could call this method *plastic reading:* a new, transformed type of structural approach. Not that it is a matter of "returning" to structuralism, "restructuring" deconstruction, or even transforming it as "poststructuralism." I believe that it is possible to claim the existence of a *structure of philosophy,* but unlike social structure, the structure of myth or kinship structures, this structure does not relate to an original or nuclear formal element, to any kind of basic cell that contains the semantic and morphological data of the system. Instead, the structure of "structural plastic analysis" should be understood as a *result,* an a posteriori structure, a *residue of history.*

The idea of a "structure of philosophy" does not therefore refer to a paradigm, model, or invariable; rather, it describes the result of the destruction and deconstruction of the paradigm, model, or invariable in general. *By "structure of philosophy," I mean the form of philosophy after its destruction and deconstruction. This means that structure is not a starting point here but rather an outcome. Structure is the order and organization of philosophy once the concepts of order and organization have themselves been deconstructed. In other words, the structure of philosophy is metamorphosized metaphysics.*

Today, no one can come unknowingly to a text by Plato, Kant, Hegel, or Nietzsche. No one can come to these texts without seeing the destruction of metaphysics. Hence no one can fail to recognize the dividing line, that Doldrums again, striating the text and opening it in two—following the bifid rule of composition for which Heidegger offers us such an in-depth analysis when he comments on the division of *The Critique of Pure Reason* into two separate volumes.[117] No one can be blind to the historical and histrial line of demarcation that separates Being from Being and in effect *structures* our approach to any given type of philosophy, including the least destructive or least deconstructive philosophy. No one. Indeed, as I tried to show in *Le Change Heidegger,* this dividing line projects its imaginary shadow over everything that exists, *including our faces,* so that they too become *transformational masks.*

Destruction and deconstruction have taken place. Now they are engaged in the plastic process of their own metamorphosis. It is no longer the time to offer "deconstructive" readings of this or that philosopher or to identify presence issues in their body or work—aside from the fact that I have never done so. Plastic reading aspires to the metamorphosis of deconstructive reading.

In *Dissemination,* Derrida establishes the rule of the "double mark" or "double fold" according to which all philosophical concepts are marked twice: once by their metaphysical meaning, then by their ultrametaphysical meaning. He writes, "every concept necessarily receives two similar marks—a repetition without identity—one mark inside and the other outside the deconstructed system."[118] Derrida's observation is exactly right, but the words "mark" and "fold" require clarification. To be more precise, it is a question of recognizing *visibility,* for the mark or fold are in fact grooves, types of relief. We must therefore discuss their *form. The plastic reading of a text is the reading that seeks to reveal the form left in the text through the withdrawing of presence, that is, through its own deconstruction.* It is a question of showing how a text *lives its deconstruction.* Not in the sense in which it would live with a graft. Plastic reading does not seek to show how the same is always already undermined, haunted, or parasited by the other; it is no longer a matter of learning to overcome the allergy or to avert rejection, nor of claiming that deconstruction is already at work in the text's self-presence. Rather, it is a matter of revealing a form in the text that is both other than the same *and* other than the other, *other than metaphysics, other than deconstruction.* A form that is the fruit of the self-regulation of the relation between tradition and its superceding and which at the same time exceeds the strict binary terms of this relation.

The Future of Hegel and *Le Change Heidegger* offer two examples of plastic reading. The first reveals an overarching structure in Hegel, constituted by the temporal deployment of subjectivity. Because of its plasticity, in different places in the system and following the dual tempo mentioned earlier, subjectivity self-regulates (it bears its accidents without dissolving) and self-engenders (it actually produces the accidents it receives). This overarching structure involves several levels of organization: anthropological, theological, and philosophical. We move from one level to the next through *differentiated sublation*, through different types and levels of *transformation*. This formal and differential structure is neither the form "in itself" of the Hegelian system—the "integrity" that is supposed to precede its destruction or its deconstruction—nor is it the result of its destruction and deconstruction. The structure refers to the *form of the system without its presence, the form of the dialectic without its metaphysical understanding*. But this form is not a mere remainder. It *relaunches itself* beyond destruction and deconstruction. It puts into play or sets off again that of which it is the form.

Conversely, in *Le Change Heidegger* an overarching structure appears, which is the metamorphic process of metaphysics, a process that takes place via three main articulations: the morphological analysis of the "first change"; the confrontation of the traditional concept and the ultrametaphysical concept of "form" within the "other change"; and, starting from a retrospective reading of "modification" in *Being and Time*, the retrospective appropriation of these different metamorphic crises by *Dasein*. In the course of the enquiry, metaphysics also shows itself as a process of self-regulation and self-engendering. Indeed, on the one hand metaphysics organizes itself: I have already emphasized Heidegger's view of the essential role of continuity for all authentic change. On the other hand, this self-regulation doubles as a process of sudden self-engendering or emergence: thanks to a leap or absolute rupture, metaphysics leaves space for the *other thing*. Once again, the two processes constitute the binary rhythm of the Heideggerian "cineplastic," the *form in double movement* mentioned earlier. This overarching structure, which is both imaginary and imaginal,[119] does not claim to be the "truth" of Heideggerian thought. Nor is it the skeleton of Heidegger's thought, that which remains of its architecture once the edifice is deconstructed or grasped by writing. Again, this form is an *answer*, an answer to Heidegger's critical posterity. It is the possible form of an other Heidegger, *of an other other thought*, launching itself beyond its own deconstruction.

Structural plastic analysis thus calls deconstruction to recognize its *metamorphic debt*. It is in this sense that it continues deconstruction, paradoxically by leading it to the most originary. The structure or form of a thought—the alterity of philosophy to both its tradition and its own destruction—is both the *specter of its history* and the outline of something within it that is *not yet born*, something *innate* in the true sense. A *childhood to come* in the text, the promise of a *primitive* stage in the text. Childhood is an age that does not belong to either metaphysics or to its superceding and that, just like "metamorphosis," is both before and after history, mythic and ultrahistorical at the same time. Childhood is the *primitive future* of texts.

It is therefore a matter of producing readings that are neither traditional nor deconstructive. Of course, this can only happen through a new writing or a new style, whose name and nature would be termed "plastic."

But to understand the inevitably metamorphosed meaning of this word, it is necessary to take the Hegelian gesture and fully complete the undertaking to delocalize the concept of plasticity outside the field of aesthetics. More specifically, it is a matter of breaking with the idea that the primary area of meaning and experience for this concept is the aesthetic or artistic field. Even more specifically, it is a matter of breaking with a particular understanding of the aesthetic or artistic field itself. The relation to form that I am trying to reveal here is both a relation to the *formal* (as ideality) and the *figural* (as corporality). But the formal is not to be confused with the suprasensitive in the first instance any more than the figural is to be confused with the figure in the second instance.

Form—formality and figurality—does not therefore open the ideologically questionable space of "ontotypology" as defined by Philippe Lacoue-Labarthe, that is, the aesthetico-poïetic function of presenting being, the incarnation of a type of exemplary *Dasein* or the fabrication of the political community on the model of the work.[120] In this interpretation, form (*Gestalt* or *Form*) is the most suspect of all metaphysical concepts. Hence the ethical necessity to give up on the scene understood as presentation, representation, or figuration. And hence the ethical necessity to privilege the formless, the unpresentable, the "defiguration," the scenic removal.

I'll readily admit that I am not convinced that this is necessary. There is an entire life, an entire destiny of form that cannot allow itself to be locked up in an alternative along the lines of "form or justice," "figure or ethics." This is the case just so far as it is impossible to saturate the field of deployment of form and figure through a restricted definition of the aesthetic and art, a definition that takes it for granted that the artistic event as thought by traditional philosophers is purely and simply a mode of *presentation,* that the mission of form would always be to convene the thing to presence, to rip it away from the secret, to make it say or incarnate, to assign it to residence in the light.

To refer only briefly to the haunting debate concerning the ethical legitimacy of images or representations of the Shoah, I simply recall that even as he lays claim to the impossibility, or even the prohibition, on representation, Lanzmann nevertheless describes his film clearly and explicitly as a *form:* the form of the "fiction of the real,"[121] the form not of images, of course, but of "imaginations." This shows that form goes far beyond the naïve type, evidence, or sensibilization of truth. Today, the aesthetic critique of form is a dominant form of ideology. Antiform is the ideological form imposed on us.

We must pay our respects here to Jean-François Lyotard for giving both the formal and the figural their true dimension as *discourse events,* in his remarkable book *Discourse, Figure.* Not once in his book are form and figure confused with either beautiful appearance or the presence of beautiful appearance. In short, form and figure are never treated as *modes of presentation.* Both terms refer rather to the *relief of language.* This does not mean that everything is language or that art is dissolved in the linguistic. Rather, it means that art is part and parcel of the depth of language; that is, art is a part of the referential function of language. The figural is the referent in as much as it is not present; *the function forms the pure spacing through which meaning is shaped:*

> It is important not to misunderstand this by concluding that there is nothing but text. The world is a function of language, but language includes a world-function; all speech constitutes that which it designates in the world, as a thick object to synthesize, a symbol to decode; but these objects and symbols present themselves in an expanse in which they can be shown, and this expanse on the edge of discourse is not itself the linguistic space in which the work of meaning takes

place, but a kind of worldly, plastic, atmospheric space in which one must move about, circle around things, to vary their silhouette and be able to offer such and such a meaning that was hitherto hidden.[122]

In this new approach to the relation between the graphic and the plastic, we can see that not only do the graphic and plastic not separate, as we already established, but furthermore, plasticity is the condition of existence of meaning in as much as it confers its *visibility* upon it, without this being confused with its presence. In this way, to borrow Lyotard's fine expression, there is "an eye at the edge of discourse."[123] This eye is the optical arrangement that language, in its structure, shows on its edge, so that to speak is to give birth to the visibility of that about which I am speaking. The eye that borders discourse certainly sees other things than discourse, but this "other thing" can only be envisaged through a discourse function. A look is inscribed originally in the speech that destines saying and seeing to each other. Thus, as Lyotard explains: "language is not a homogenous milieu; it is divisive because it exteriorizes the sensible opposite itself."[124]

Visibility thus defined is "an exteriority that cannot be interiorized as *signification*."[125] This exteriority is also the space that belongs to the art whose operating involves going "from the interior of discourse . . . into the figure."[126] As Lyotard says, "the [artistic] figure is a deformation that imposes another form on the arrangement of linguistic units." This other form is a pure energy "which folds, which crumples and creases the text and makes a work from it, a difference."[127] And isn't this energy, infinitely composed in painting, fiction, music, and poetry, precisely *the form of writing*?[128]

It is important to further examine this gesture to "deaesthetize form"—thanks to which, paradoxically, it gains all its artistic significance—in order to see in the figural not a means of plastic resistance to discourse but the depth of the field of discourse itself. I mean that the "figural," or plasticity, can now refer to the open gap in philosophical discourse between its traditional or "metaphysical" form and its "deconstructed" form. In the gaping openness of the face-off between these two forms, a new *figural-textual* depth is created, a space where plastic reading can get to work.

To philosophize today can no longer consist in restituting texts within a totalizing history or substituting a series of pure gaps for historical teleology, as if traditional texts were simple fragments or "shards" of meaning. The figural structure that we must try to reveal in texts is not a constraining framework or potential dispersive space; rather, it is a matter of causing the form that comes *after presence* to arise in works.

XIII. ON PLASTICITY AS A MOTOR SCHEME

In the light of what I have said, it should be clear that plasticity refers to both a new mode of being of form and a new grasp of this mode of being itself, in other words, a new *scheme*.

What I termed a "motor scheme" earlier is not, strictly speaking, the "spirit" of an era or the "form of a consciousness." Yet form and scheme present themselves to a certain consciousness and a certain era as hermeneutic instruments, privileged reading approaches of their self-analysis. And, as I have said, the concept of plasticity is becoming both the dominant formal motif of interpretation and the most productive exegetical and heuristic tool of our time.

First, this is because *plasticity is the systemic law of the deconstructed real*, a mode of organization of the real that comes after metaphysics and that is appearing today in all the different domains of human activity. In *Le Change Heidegger*, I tried to define this new configuration as *an ultrahistorical configuration of the world, a mode of transformation following history*. Today, *new metamorphic occurrences* are appearing at the level of social and economic organization and at the level of "gender" or individual sexual identity. From the start I have said that the privileged regime of change today is the continuous implosion of form, through which it recasts and reforms itself continually.

Then also because we can only access these new organizations or configurations thanks to a tool that *conforms to these forms* itself, a tool that accords with them or is adequate to them, *and this is no longer the case with writing*.

Why? The constitution of writing as a motor scheme was the result of a gradual movement that began with structuralism and found its mooring in linguistics, genetics, and cybernetics. A pure linguistic image, the image of the gap or difference, gradually established itself as the scheme of an ontological organization.

The impact of a book such as François Jacob's *The Logic of Life* extended, even if not explicitly, Lévi-Strauss's conclusions about linguistics: it is the theoretical expression of a certain organization of the real, a global morphology made up of "meaningful gaps" and differences. *The Logic of Life* confirmed the existence of this linguistic structure of being by privileging the role of writing within it. In effect, the genetic *code* then became a true ontological motif. The "standard" meaning of writing was thus in the process of "widening." Jacob's book bears witness to the extension of the graphic scheme beyond genetic boundaries. DNA is the biological translation of a general ontology of the graph. "Any material structure can . . . be compared to a message," Jacob declares.[129] The concepts of genetic coding or writing witness the fact that the graph was in the process of establishing itself as the privileged hermeneutic image and instrument of an era.

In this graph ontology, the origin—whatever meaning is attributed to this word—can only be thought in terms of a trace, that is, a difference to the self. Generally, it is the concept of *program*—which is obviously also a concept in the field of cybernetics—that culminates and completes the constitution of the graphic scheme as the motor scheme of thought. Derrida alone recognized the full importance of this fulfillment and culmination:

> Now we tend to say "writing" for all that and more: to designate not only the physical gestures of literal pictographic or ideographic inscription, but also the totality of what makes it possible; and also, beyond the signifying face, the signified face itself. And thus we say "writing" for all that gives rise to an inscription in general, whether it is literal or not and even if what it distributes in space is alien to the order of the voice: cinematography, choreography, of course, but also pictorial, musical, sculptural "writing." One might also speak of athletic writing, and with even greater certainty of military or political writing in view of the techniques that govern those domains today. All this to describe not only the system of notation secondarily connected with these activities but the essence and the content of these activities themselves. It is also in this sense that the

contemporary biologist speaks of writing and *pro-gram* in relation to the most elementary processes of information within the living cell.[130]

Derrida describes here the *semantic enlargement* of the concept of writing, not as an arbitrary philosophical decision but as an event, the appearance of a new order, starting from the pregnancy of the motifs of program, information, or code. It is only on the basis of this programmatic organization of the real as it is liable to come to the awareness of an era that writing was able to constitute itself as a *philosophical* motor scheme.

Yet today we must acknowledge that the power of the linguistic-graphic scheme is diminishing and that it has entered a twilight for some time already. It now seems that plasticity is slowly but surely establishing itself as the paradigmatic figure of organization in general.

Considering cerebral plasticity in my book *What Should We Do with Our Brain?*, I studied the most convincing example. In his well-known book *Neuronal Man: The Biology of Mind*, Jean-Pierre Changeux reproaches philosophers for not showing enough interest in recent discoveries about neuronal functioning. He claims that this lack of interest is indicative of an unacceptable ignorance about, or scorn for, the extraordinary revolution produced by brain research in the twentieth century. "In the last twenty years, our knowledge in this field [the neurosciences] has undergone an expansion matched only by the growth of physics at the beginning of the century and molecular biology in the 1950s. The impact of the discovery of the synapse and its functions is comparable to that of the atom or DNA."[131]

The "plasticity" of the brain refers to the capacity of synapses to modify their transmission effectiveness. Synapses are not in fact frozen; to this degree, they are not mere transmitters of nerve information but, in a certain sense, they have the power to *form* or *reform* information. This type of plasticity makes it possible to forward the hypothesis of neuronal circuits that are able to self-organize, that is, to modify their connections during the activity required by perception or learning.

According to Changeux, there is no question that above all else "the exceptional . . . plasticity of human cerebral organization" is the most worthy object of philosophical reflection.[132] Indeed, thanks to the fundamental discoveries of neurobiology, "we [now] have physical traces of the accessing of meaning."[133] This statement is crucial. The "traces" that Changeux is referring to here are in fact first and foremost *images* and *forms*. In fact, new technologies of medical imagery make it possible to observe the human brain at work. When used in conjunction with electrical recordings of the brain, these techniques are a major contribution to research about the cerebral zones underlying specific elements of mental activity. We are now even able to photograph the double mode of coding of behaviors (perceptive or other): both the topology of nerve connections and the journeys of their corresponding impulses. The result of this double coding is called the *graph*.[134]

Yet paradoxically, this *graph* is not a writing; this trace *does not proceed by printing or facilitation*. Hence, the metaphor used to describe it *is not a graphic metaphor*. Instead, the metaphor used is the geographic or political metaphor of *assemblies, forms,* or *neuronal populations*. As Changeux writes: "the concept of assemblies or cooperative groups of neurons leads directly from one level of organization to another, from the individual neuron to a population of neurons."[135] These assemblies therefore determine the appearance of graphs. The model of *re-formation* or *re-composition* replaces the model of *facilitation:* "It becomes plausible that such assemblies, made up of oscillatory neurons with high *spontaneous* activity, could recombine among themselves."[136] "Linkages," "relationships," and "spider's webs" are some of the *configurations* taken by nerve information networks. Thus it appears that synaptic fissures are certainly gaps, but they are *gaps that are able to form or take shape*. That's it, in fact: *traces take form*. It is striking to note that neuronal plasticity—in other words, the ability of synapses to modify their effectiveness as a result of experience—is a part of genetic indetermination. We can therefore make the claim that *plasticity forms where DNA no longer writes*.

EPILOGUE

Since *The Future of Hegel,* I have considered plasticity constantly from both the philosophical and the scientific perspective. The two approaches, ontological—developed particularly in *Le Change Heidegger*—and epistemological—the emphasis on the pregnancy of the concept of plasticity in neurobiology and the cognitive sciences—consistently confirmed my intuition that plasticity, as a motor scheme, was in the process of taking over from writing.

I believe that I have shown how, from a philosophical point of view, plasticity refers both to the process of temporization at work in the heart of subjectivity (Hegel) and absolute ontological exchangeability (Heidegger) and also how, from the scientific viewpoint, plasticity characterizes a regime of systematic self-organization that is based on the ability of an organism to integrate the modifications that it experiences and to modify them in return. Considered from these two philosophical and epistemological points of view (they are not the only possible viewpoints), plasticity is able to *momentarily characterize the material organization of thought and being*. It is my opinion therefore that we should certainly be engaging deconstruction in a *new materialism*.

The plastic bond unifies the self-organization of subjectivity (Hegel's temporization), the economy of ontological exchangeability (Heidegger's transformation), and the constitution of momentary, always metamorphosable, always transformable configurations, which constitute the architecture of thought (the synaptic organization). Finally, the *other form* participates in these three models simultaneously, without being reduced to them, and borrows its renewed vitality from these three dynamics. It does not immobilize itself and does not present itself; it remains as a mobile, and therefore precarious, gathering. The link, binder, and synthesis are all plastic today; they are both resistant and fragile, solid and ready to break up—and the political consequences of this statement must be considered. I would like to continue to show that plasticity *configures traces and erases them to form them, without however rigidifying them*. In this sense, plasticity appears clearly *at the dusk of writing*.

The dusk of writing. Dusk is a time of reprieve. Dusk is a time of mourning. Dusk is a time of melancholy. Dusk is a time of separation. Dusk is a time of metamorphosis. I translate: plasticity is the reprieve of writing; plasticity is the mourning of writing; plasticity is the melancholy of writing; plasticity is the separation from writing; plasticity is the metamorphosis of writing.

Yet because any statement is split in half, dislocated by its own difference to itself, its own aphoristic or graphic force, I might just as well say that the mourning of writing is impossible or the reprieve of writing is impossible, as is its metamorphosis. That in this dusk of our own, there is nothing but melancholy, the sadness of an impossible separation. I believe that one side of me, of my mask, will always remain caught between "no" and "no," between dialectic and deconstruction, certainty and uncertainty about the power of the solution. *But despite it all,* another side leans toward a dusk that is the dusk of farewell; *despite it all,* another side leans toward the reprieve, or at least toward a degree of success in mourning.

Let us return to Lévi-Strauss in closing, as it all started with him. He admits that initially he did not understand the meaning of transformational masks: "Their plastic justification escaped me," he says. "They were made to be worn in front of the face, yet they had only slightly concave backs that did not really follow the relief.... Why this unusual shape, so ill-adapted to their function? Why the gaping mouth? . . . [and] enormous tongue?" A little later on, he gives the answer: "I was unable to answer any of these questions until I realized that, as is the case with myths, masks, too, cannot be interpreted in and by themselves as separate objects."[137] Thus a mask, like a myth, only acquires meaning "once it is put back in the group of its transformations." From one culture to another, from one people to another, strangely, masks answer each other, reply, changing their curve or color, keeping the overarching form of the series even as they take on a sovereign individuality.

I tell myself that the law of motor schemes is the same: from graphic to plastic, the meaning of pure images can only be caught in the light of their mutual transformations. Meaning—why that's metamorphosis.

Paris–New York–Paris
Fall 2003–Fall 2004

Afterword

OF THE IMPOSSIBILITY OF FLEEING—PLASTICITY

To explain why *Plasticity at the Dusk of Writing* is both an autobiography and a conceptual portrait, I will talk about the impossibility of fleeing. The impossibility of fleeing where flight, however, would appear to be the obvious and only solution. The impossibility of fleeing in those moments when an extreme tension, a pain, a sensation of uneasiness surges toward an outside that does not exist. Something that is so constituted as to make fleeing impossible while also making it necessary to flee this impossibility. What is a "way out"; what could a "way out" be when there is no outside, no "elsewhere"? It is not a question of how to escape closure but rather of how to escape within closure itself.

The drive is for Freud the privileged example of this strange situation, the specific excitation that cannot find its discharge outside of the psyche: "We thus arrive at the essential nature of drives in the first place by considering their main characteristics—their origin in the sources of stimulation within the organism and their appearance as a constant source—and from this we deduce one of their further features, namely that no actions of flight avail against them."[1] The question indeed is how then to "eliminate" this constant force. Freud states: "that which follows is an attempt at flight—the formation of the phobia."[2] The only possible solution to the impossibility of fleeing would thus be formation or transformation, that is to say, in the first place, the constitution of closure in a

AFTERWORD

form that changes it into an equivalent of flight, by way of bypassing, avoiding, and displacing the prohibition of transition or transgression.

This structure, the structure of the formation of a pathway as a "way out" in the absence of a "way out" is central to my book. I name "plasticity" the logic and the economy of such a formation: the movement of the constitution of an exit, there, where no such exit is possible. To put it differently, plasticity renders possible the appearance or formation of alterity where the other is absent. Plasticity is the form of alterity without transcendence.

My usage of plasticity addresses the issue of the Other and of the outside in late twentieth-century Continental philosophy. For Levinas, the alterity of the utterly other, the foundation of ethics, would in effect always have to take place on the outside. The encounter with the other, the response to the moral injunction, would always have to occur "elsewhere," to the extent that the very movement of the encounter in general, which Levinas calls "metaphysics," is a move toward "somewhere else." At the beginning of *Totality and Infinity*, he presents a conception of metaphysical desire that absolutely opposes the Freudian definition of the drive:

> In the most general form it has assumed in the history of thought [metaphysics] appears as a movement going forth from a world that is familiar to us, whatever be the yet unknown lands that bound it or that hides it from view, from an "at home" which we inhabit, toward an alien outside-of-oneself, toward a yonder. The term of this movement, the elsewhere or the other, is called *other* in an eminent sense. No journey, no change of climate or of scenery could satisfy the desire bent toward it. The other metaphysically desired is not "other" like the bread I eat, the land in which I dwell, the landscape I contemplate.... I can "feed" on these realities and to a very great extent satisfy myself, as though I had simply been lacking them. Their *alterity* is thereby reabsorbed into my own identity as a thinker or a possessor. The metaphysical desire tends toward *something else entirely*, toward the *absolutely other*.[3]

But where there is no outside, how can one reach toward the other, how can one respond to the other? How can the psyche endure the constant pressure of a call without exteriority or transcendence? How can one form the pathway; how can one work out a form of flight toward the other from within the closure of the world? *Plasticity designates the form of a world without any exteriority, a world in which the other appears as utterly other precisely because she is not someone else.*

Why is the concept of plasticity able to help us think of the formation of a "way out," of an alterity that does not come from a yonder? The noun "plasticity" is linked etymologically with two older words, the substantive "plastic" and the adjective "plastic." All three words are derived from the Greek *plassein*, which means "to model" or "to mold." "Plastic" as an adjective has two meanings. On the one hand, it means "to be susceptible to changes of form" or "to be malleable." Clay, in this sense, would be "plastic." On the other hand, it means "having the power to bestow form," as in the expression "plastic surgeon" or "plastic art" understood as "the art of modeling" in the arts of sculpture or ceramics. Plasticity describes the nature of that which is plastic, being at once capable of receiving and of giving form.

We have certainly not yet exhausted plasticity's range of meanings, which continues to evolve with and in language. One might think, for example, of all the various forms of "plastic" in our world: plastic wood, plastic money, plastic paint, and the dangerous plastic material of putty-like consistency that can be shaped by hand. The very significance of plasticity itself appears to be plastic, mapped somewhere between two extremes. On the one hand, plasticity may be used to describe the crystallization of form and the concretization of shape—as is suggested by the terms plastic as a substance and plastic art as modeling. On the other hand, plasticity appears diametrically opposed to form, describing the destruction and the very annihilation of all form—as suggested by the term "plastic" explosive for a bomb.

To think of the formation of a way out in the absence of a way out, within the closure, is to think about an immanent disruption, a sudden transformation without any change of ground, a mutation that produces a new form of identity and makes the former one explode. This mutation is like the opening or closing of a "transformational mask."

Fleeing without going anywhere else is in every case a question of the possibility of transformation and metamorphosis. As it already and very clearly appears in the work of Ovid, metamorphosis—both the receiving and giving of form—has always been thought, as Freud precisely puts it, as "the formation of an attempt at flight." The *Metamorphoses* of Ovid stage certain moments when the changing of form is the only way to escape danger. Daphne, for example, is able to escape Apollo only by changing herself into a tree. This moment of transformation is also a moment of destruction: the giving of form goes hand in hand with its suppression. All that remains of the former body is a heart that beats for a while under the bark, or some tears which quickly dry. The formation of a new individual is indeed this explosion of form, an explosion that clears the way and allows the pursuer at the same time to suddenly recognize irreducible otherness.

For some years now in my work I have been concentrating on characterizing the moment when the motif of metamorphosis stops designating a merely mythological or fictitious reality in order to take on an ontological sense, explicitly in the history of philosophy. In so doing, I have been tracing the history of the development of the concept of plasticity starting with the philosophy of Hegel, where I encountered this concept for the first time. Plasticity in Hegel characterizes the internal mobility of the system. I then progressed to the thought of Heidegger, for whom metamorphosis no longer refers solely to an accidental possibility or a resource for fiction but rather to the very movement of being.

In *Being and Time*, Heidegger clearly puts the world in touch with the absence of any outside-of-the-world. Being-in-the-world, existing, amounts to experiencing an absence of exteriority, which is equally an absence of interiority. There is neither an inside nor an outside of the world. Dasein transcends itself, or in other words, ex-ists, only in the absence of a way out. To exist is thus neither to enter nor to leave but rather to cross thresholds of transformation. Dasein, says Heidegger, transcends itself only by becoming modified. This is the concept of modification that, in *Being and Time*, sets up an economy of plasticity. Every adventure, every crossing, every experience, death itself, "must be understood" as "a modification of the primordial being-in [*Modifikation des ursprünglichen In-Seins*]."[4]

Dasein, to say it again, is a "structural whole."[5] This structure is "articulated" (*gegliedert*) in various modes of being. Now, it is the passage from one mode of being to another, for example from the mode of "taking care of things" to that of "concern," which occurs via modification. The structural whole is mobile and differentiated, but it cannot be shattered. It is thus by successive transformations that Dasein passes from one manner of being to another. Modification can be radical, violent; it can completely and utterly transform Dasein, "drastically changing him," says Heidegger. And yet Dasein remains a whole. Modification does not bring about fragmentation. It may mark the worst of disagreements of Dasein with himself, the most serious of conflicts, yet modification does not shatter Dasein. Dasein's structural unity, declares Heidegger, resists "the most fatal tendencies to divide it up."[6]

Modification describes precisely the mobility that characterizes an infrangible structure, one that cannot break out of itself. This structure is finite, absolutely exposed, but ontologically whole. Modification of structure is always and necessarily modification within the structure.

In this way, both disorientation and the "fall,"[7] which are analyzed by Heidegger precisely in terms of "flight," are only modifications of being-in-the-world: "In falling... nothing other than our potentiality for being-in-the-world is the issue, even if in the mode of inauthenticity."[8] It is the same for the passage to authentic existence: "On the other hand authentic existence is nothing which hovers over entangled everydayness, but is existentially only a modified grasp of everydayness."[9] Neither inside nor outside nor high nor low, that which comes to pass, that which occurs, does so unexpectedly only by means of modification, by way of transformation. In this way, a mode emerges only from the modification of another. One mode gives way to another plastically, forming a new possibility.

Every effect of absolute otherness (outside or inside of the world) is, as modification, the result of a "concealment," "a covering up," or a "veiling."[10] In the same way, the "call" of moral conscience does not resonate from a place of absolute exteriority or of absolute transcendence but rather becomes understood as a modification, that is, the transformation of inauthentic potentiality-of-being.

Heidegger writes: "The 'world' at hand does not become 'another world,' the circle of the others is not exchanged for a new one."¹¹

Crossing thresholds without changing ground, being able neither to transgress nor to shut oneself in, only hiding or exposing oneself. Experiencing otherness starting with the defeat of any alterity of pure transcendence—without the possibility of an exit. Such is the condition of the plasticity of existence.

Modification makes possible a kind of indentation in the very absence of recess, which lets the other in, where the other runs out. This opening is that of the formative decision, as Jean-Luc Nancy says in his essay "The Decision of Existence."¹² He shows that authentic and inauthentic are, according to Heidegger, "two different ways of being the same subject." For Dasein, deciding, that is, making up one's own mind for oneself, cannot reside in escaping inauthenticity.

> Decision decides neither in favor of nor by virtue of any "authenticity" whereby the world of existence would be surmounted or transfigured in any way whatsoever. The decision is made (it grasps itself, is grasped by itself, surprises itself) right in ontical experience, and it opens to ontical experience. In fact, there is no other experience, and only in illusion could our decision claim to decide for and within another "world" (and yet even illusion is part of experience . . .). Ontical experience takes place right at the "they," and nowhere else. Moreover, there is no "elsewhere": that is the "meaning [*Sinn*] of Being.¹³

We can see, once again, that authenticity is only a modified, transformed grasp of existence. There is no change of ground. The "way out" is achieved by an upheaval within daily existence itself.

Consequently, the plasticity of existence signifies that Dasein has to be held always between the birth and the destruction of possibilities, between the emergence and destruction of forms of being, without ever being able to flee the responsibility of this middle course, this in-between. When plasticity is taken into account, it becomes possible to deconstruct the substantive appearance of existence and to think of identity as something mobile, whose many frontiers, psychic as well as political, are constantly being drawn, erased, redrawn, and negotiated. Fleeing frontiers is simply not an option. In this way, existence would be the plastic drive within the closed form of the world, within the closure of globalization.

I. PLASTICITY AND HOSPITALITY

A. From Heidegger to Kafka

At this point, we come across the major objection that Levinas raises against plasticity. To affirm the closure of existence: is that not in effect to compromise the very possibility of the relation to the other? To be altered: is that not to continue to remain within oneself? Is not the Heideggerian conception of *Mitsein*, a community without transcendence, another form of identitarianism? To give another form to the solitude of this "oneself"? Can we not say that alterity, in its very concept, exceeds every register of form or of formation? To consider existence as plastic, as I am doing: is that not to refuse the irreducible reality of the alterity within it?

Kafka's book *Metamorphosis* appears to demonstrate this danger. Indeed, the beetle Samsa might be seen as a being that can no longer be modified because of modification itself, "metamorphosis" naming paradoxically the impossibility of metamorphosis. When it comes down to it, is it not the case that a being that is transformed is, at the same time, forever deprived of the possibility of changing, of altering itself?

Would he not be condemned to live in a world that is nothing more than a room? A confined world, a set of doors that never gives access to anything except other rooms and other doors in the world? This sentiment of routine, of the repetition of the same, is perhaps the only possible sentiment of existence, the sentiment of the incessant. Blanchot would be able to say that effectively the same goes for Dasein as for Samsa:

> Gregor's state is the very state of being that cannot withdraw from existence, and for which existing means being forever condemned to descend into existence. Turned into a vermin, he carries on living in the mode of "the fall," he sinks into

animal solitude, and he gets closer, as near as possible, to the absurdity and the impossibility of living. But what happens? He continues, precisely, to live.[14]

On this point, Blanchot and Levinas affirm that transcendence is the act and the affirmation of singular existence by which the existent can break with the permanent essence of existing. At the same time, by means of such a rupture, the existent also breaks with form and with plasticity.

B. Globalization Versus Cosmopolitanism?

A major current political issue concerns the possibility of reconfiguring a conception of the international such that it is no longer coterminous with the economic determination of globalization. The term to be used to identify this possibility might be "cosmopolitan."

The critical articulation of "cosmopolitanism" and "globalization" has already received a response. Levinas and Derrida, in particular, have thought them out by way of the problem of *hospitality*.

The concept of hospitality immediately makes the difference between cosmopolitanism and globalization resonate. Cosmopolitanism, defined by Kant as the possibility for man to become a citizen of the world, implies an ethics of the unconditional welcome of the other. Unlike globalization, cosmopolitanism would refer to the logic of an impossible identitarian hegemony, the impossible closing in on the self, or in other words, the logic of a hospitable self-other relation, defined as "dwelling" [*l'habitation*].

For Levinas, it is the whole of subjectivity itself that is defined as, and by means of, the welcome of the other. The other is originally more present to me than my own self, and this is why hospitality highlights above all else the ontological reality of an otherness older than identity, a reality that prevents any closure of the identity on its own self. In *Adieu to Emmanuel Levinas*, Derrida declares: "The subject is a host [*hôte*],"[15] which means also that the subject is a "hostage."[16] The subject comes after the other, answering *to* her answering *for* her. Derrida goes on: "the host is a hostage insofar as he is a subject put into question, obsessed (and thus besieged), persecuted, in the very place where he takes place [*dans le lieu même où il a lieu*], where, as emigrant, exile, stranger, a guest [*hôte*] from the beginning, he finds himself elected to or taken up by a residence before himself electing or taking one up."[17] Playing with the double meaning of the French word *hôte*, which can signify both host and guest, Derrida says once more that "we must be reminded of this implacable law of hospitality: the *hôte* who receives (the host), the one who welcomes the invited or received *hôte* (the guest), the welcoming *hôte* who considers himself the owner of the place [*propriétaire des lieux*], is in truth a *hôte* received in his own home."[18]

If cosmopolitanism cannot merge with globalization, it is because far from originating in a substantial self-sufficiency, cosmopolitanism on the contrary responds in its organization to a visit, the very first visit of the other person. The transcendental memory of this first visit destines cosmopolitanism to be a nonfinite opening. For Levinas and Derrida alike, this mark carries the name *trace*. Cosmopolitanism responds in its structure to the ethical injunction of the past as the fact of the other's passage [*passage*], that is, as the "trace."

It is clear that hospitality, which also engages a design of the trace, is thought by Levinas and Derrida alike as a counter to plasticity, as a counterplasticity. Both in its concept and in its concrete implementation, hospitality is not plastic. That is, hospitality in no way obeys the receiving and the bestowing of form. It does not obey the annihilation of form either. Both in its appearance and its destruction alike, form always appears to shut out otherness, to reify it, to reduce otherness to presence and evidence of the same. Form, in this sense, would always be the sign of a refusal to welcome. On principle, a form would not be hospitable; it would remain of the order of self-identity even when it explodes: terrorism is always identitarian. In other words, hospitality defines the ethical and political place where form and trace are separated.

This separation may be described as a dissociation, as Derrida describes it when he speaks of modern architecture's "concern for the impossible." "To accede to the dissociation but to implement it as such in the space of a gathering together."[19] To dissociate within the gathering: this would be the injunction of hospitality, a command to which plasticity could not respond.

"Beneath form," says Levinas, "things conceal themselves."[20] Hospitality implies the possibility to have access to such a "beneath." For its part, deconstruction signifies also, first and foremost, the deconstruction of form.

One could say, however, that deconstruction would have found, in plasticity, its most faithful expression, the conceptual *hôte*—both host *and* guest—most worthy of the concept of hospitality. For is not plastic the substitutable material par excellence? Can it not take the place of every thing, can it not deconstruct every idea of authenticity, is it not always engaged in the process of its own disappearance? Is it not always beyond its very own form because it can change?

But no, we must draw attention to this fact: the plastic has never appealed to the philosophers. Roland Barthes alone devoted a short chapter of *Mythologies* to it. Plastic, according to him, embodies "the very idea of... infinite transformation." Possessing endless possibilities, with a protean ability to assume any imaginable shape, plastic's "proliferating forms of matter" trigger perpetual amazement. Barthes warns, however, that plastic's ability to become anything at all may reduce anything to nothing by dissolving all differences. He concludes that, with the advent of plastic as a universal solvent, "the hierarchy of substances is abolished: a single one replaces them all: the whole world can be plasticized."[21] I think that Barthes's worry regarding plastic's ability to dissolve differences can be widened to relate to hospitality in general. Because plasticity never presents itself without form, plastic is always thought as a factor of identification, standardization, or globalization and never as a possible welcome of the other.

We must conclude, then, that hospitality necessarily and resolutely involves a principle of antiplastic protection, which allows it to keep otherness beyond the reach of form. Form would run the risk of destroying transcendence by integrating it into a synthetic whole or a systemic closure. Hospitality is the political weapon against plasticity, understood as the global and capitalistic economy of the world.

II. PLASTICITY AND THE "MESSIANIC"

In *A Time for Farewell*, Derrida clearly presents his philosophical resistance to plasticity. This text is a very subtle and generous response to my book *The*

AFTERWORD

Future of Hegel: Plasticity, Temporality, and Dialectic. In this book, I show that for Hegel "plasticity" characterizes the relationship between the subject and its accidents and consequently between subjectivity and temporality. The subject is said to be "plastic" to the extent that it both anticipates and does not know what is coming or happening to it. Derrida answers that what is to come would always happen "from *behind* or *vertically,* from a very high stance, in truth from the height of a height much higher than height itself or any height whatsoever."[22] This mode of occurring would deceive any plastic horizon of anticipation or expectation. Derrida often thinks of it in terms of "the messianic," that is, of a "messianicity without messianism." In *Faith and Knowledge,* he writes: "First name: the *messianic,* or messianicity without messianism. This would be the opening to the future or to the coming of the other as the advent of justice, but without horizon of expectation and without prophetic prefiguration."[23]

In *A Time for Farewells,* he pursues: "I am not letting only one theologian speak, I am not only allowing for the one preoccupied by the transcendence of an Absolute Other which we do not see."[24] However, the nonplastic mode of expectation would resist any kind of presence and face-to-face relationship with the event or the "arrivant"; it would oppose any reduction of the event itself to a temporal form or shape.

> This event can or may come from that which is the highest but it may also come from "behind," from what comes and comes back from behind me, always, as if it came in my back, from behind my back, without ever presenting in front of me, not even as the face of the other: the coming of an event which, to have taken place, would never present itself, has never presented itself and will never present itself. It would come to me, this event, if we are entitled to believe it can or may come *to me,* not only without prevision or without being called or recalled to my attention, but without even presenting itself *to me*.[25]

Unrecognizable as such, as if in disguise or even nonexisting—if by existing we mean a material presence—the event would forever remain irreducible to form. Just like God, a nondialectical and "nonplastic" God, who would resist his own "plastification."[26] Who would be such a God? Derrida answers:

75

AFTERWORD

Because God remains himself still to come, should not his death, if it has ever taken place, be *purely* accidental? Absolutely unpredictable and never reappropriable, never re-essentializable, not even by some endless work of mourning, not even, and above all, by God himself? A God who would have, without ever seeing it come, let an infinite bomb explode in his hands, a God dead by some hopeless accident, hopeless of any salvation or redemption, without essentializing *sublation,* without any work of mourning and without any possible return or refund, would that be the condition of a future, if there must be such a thing called the future? The very condition for something to come, and even that of another God, of an absolute other God?"[27]

This "accidental" utterly other God cannot take any form, cannot appear as the result of a metamorphosis. Again, his nonplastic mode of being is that of trace, or of writing. The "messianic" is very close to writing and trace. In *"Différance,"* Derrida affirms:

> Since the trace is not a presence but the simulacrum of a presence that dislocates itself, displaces itself, refers itself, it properly has no site. Erasure belongs to its structure. And not only the erasure which must always be able to overtake it (without which it would not be a trace but an indestructible and monumental substance), but also the erasure which constitutes it from the outset as a trace, which situates it as the change of site, and makes it disappear in its appearance, makes it emerge from itself in its production.[28]

III. PLASTICITY AND MATERIALITY

Why then, do I constantly affirm the impossibility of any transcendence, of any "disappearance in appearance," of any messianicity? Why do I affirm the political, theological, and ontological resistance of plasticity? Why do I state that plasticity survives or transgresses its own deconstruction?

In this book, I comment on Levinas's expression "the trace is inconvertible into forms," stating that if the trace is inconvertible, then it acquires the status of

AFTERWORD

a substance or a fetish. The assertion of inconvertibility lies, for Marx, at the heart of fetishism. On the face of it, the fetish always occurs outside the operation of exchange, outside the market. From then on, when otherness is fetishized by its resistance to plasticity, when hospitality continues to be thought as the "counter" to plasticity or, in other words, against form, it is no longer possible to distinguish cosmopolitanism rigorously from hypercapitalism.

Thinking out the relation between cosmopolitanism and globalization thus requires thinking out another sort of relation between hospitality, on the one hand, and form and convertibility, on the other—a relation within which nothing escapes transformation or the operation of exchange. We need, in the wake of deconstruction, to bring the trace up to date. In a manner that would prevent the trace's nondeconstructed sanctification, we need to think out more carefully the relation between the trace and form, and more specifically, the nature of the trace's necessary convertibility into form.

To state that nothing is unconvertible amounts to claiming the philosophical necessity of the thought of a new materialism, which does not believe in the "formless" and implies the vision of a malleable real that challenges the conception of time as a purely messianic process. It means that we can sometimes decide about the future (as I suggest in my book, *What Should We Do with Our Brain?*),[29] which means that there is actually something to do with it, in the sense in which Marx says that men make their own history.

This new materialist/plastic vision of time, which no longer opposes trace to form, lays a new foundation for a revised notion of ontological difference and provides a new epoch for what Derrida calls the "supplement," replacing grammatology with neurology.

A. A New Approach to Ontological Difference

What are these new ontological principles? Exploring the problematic of "modification" in *Being and Time* led me to situate the crux and motor of Heidegger's thought in originary transformation. The question of Being conceals that of change (*Wandel, Wandlung, Verwandlung:* change, transformation, metamorphosis), understood in both its immediate and more latent economic senses: alteration, exchange, convertibility, substitution. From metaphysics to what Heidegger, in *Contributions to Philosophy*, calls "the other thinking," Being is nothing ... but its mutability. A power of metamorphosis entailing an absolute exchangeability between all things, a general economy that, because it lacks a stable or common currency, is a trade in essences and not just their deconstruction.

Who or what is now coming with such change, and how are we going to be transformed now that history is over? In what metamorphoses, migrations, and revolutions will we really be engaged? At the moment of technologically conditioned sexual, biological, and political self-fashioning, at the moment of the plasticity of all identity, these questions find their fantastic actuality. An entirely new vision of difference can thus take form, as long as philosophy faces up to the growing pains of its current mutation.

To read Heidegger from the perspective of such ontological mutability and exchange challenges assumptions that the difference between Being and beings is rigid and unchangeable. The metaphysical tradition being definable as the long history of a substitution—that of being(s) for Being—both Being and being(s) are therefore transformable, transposable instances that can wear each other's masks. If this is true, Heidegger's announcement of the "other thought" corresponds to the coming of a new type of exchange and mutual transformability between Being and beings and certainly not to the disappearance of this substitutability.

The time has come to reevaluate the role of beings in Heidegger and desacralize the ontological difference so as to understand how beings—unstable, contingent, accidental beings, precisely what comes up short in regards to the essential—can and always will come to furnish the very essence of Being.

The mutability of beings is what opens a future in the absence of any openness of the world.

B. Grammatology and Neurology

The trace is no longer a suitable scheme to express and describe such a mutability. The substitution of plasticity for imprint or trace in the current scientific description of the nervous system is an interesting and fundamental path to follow in order to understand the current becoming-obsolete of "trace" or "writing." Did Derrida ever consider the possible caducity of the graphic model in general? Certainly he states that a supplement exists only inside a chain of substitutions, thus seeming to admit that the supplement "writing" could abandon its place to another. However, this structure of substitution remains above all and according to him integrable in the working of writing, and the historical emergence of *another supplementarity*—for instance, plastic—in no way invalidates the fact that history is a form of writing in its very principle:

> that historicity itself is tied to the possibility of writing; to the possibility of writing in general, beyond those particular forms of writing in the name of which we have long spoken of peoples without writing and without history. Before being the object of a history—of a historical science—writing opens the field of history—of historical becoming.... The history of writing should turn back toward the origin of historicity.[30]

This means that writing has the capacity to incorporate the historically *nongrammatological character of its supplements*. In my view, however, writing does not have this capacity. There is in fact a power of fabrication of meaning that exceeds the graphic sign. This nongraphic supplement does not introduce a logocentric residue, but it marks the *difference of the grammatological instance from itself*, which is also its twilight.

Indeed, it seems that from now on plasticity imposes itself, gradually but surely, as the pervading figure of the system of the real in general. The brain's plasticity presents a model of organization that can still be described in terms of an imprint economy, but neuronal traces don't proceed as do writing traces: *they do not leave a trace;* they occur as *changes of form.*

IV. WITHIN THE CLOSURE

In *The Moses of Michelangelo*,[31] Freud puts the impossibility of fleeing in touch with plastic art or modeling. In carving Moses, Michelangelo gives form to the fact that the patriarch was unable to give free rein to his anger faced with the idolatrous attitude of the Hebrews, unable to simply leave, unable to leave them to themselves. Moses would like to break the Tables of the Law, to leap up, to give vent to his rage, to take revenge. But Michelangelo has chosen to carve him at the very moment that he masters his fury and remains seated.

> The Moses we have reconstructed will never leap up nor cast the Tables from him. What we see before us is not the inception of a violent action but the remains of a movement that has already taken place. In his first transport of fury, Moses desired to act, to spring up and take vengeance and forget the Tables, but he has overcome the temptation, and he will now remain seated and still, in his subdued rage and in his pain mingled with contempt.[32]

Further on, Freud tells us that Michelangelo has added "something new and more than human to the figure of Moses; so that the giant frame with his tremendous physical power becomes only a concrete expression of the highest mental achievement that is possible in a man, that of struggling successfully against an inward passion for the sake of a cause to which he has devoted himself."[33]

Moses does not get up, he spurns neither the Tables nor his people, and he does not flee. He remains seated, but this position, far from being passive, conveys, Freud says, the most powerful, the most profound of transformations: the possibility of rising above his own nature and of thus opening himself to alterity, restoring his divine mission, by means of this psychical gesture of reshaping identity. Ethical plasticity is thus indeed what one can call the sculpture or carving of the other into the rock of his absence.

Slavoj Žižek perfectly understands and describes what is politically at stake in such an analysis. In *The Parallax View*, he writes:

> At its most elementary, freedom is not the freedom to do as you like (that is, to follow your inclinations without any externally imposed constraints), but to do what you don't want to do, to thwart the "spontaneous" realization of an impetus. This is the link between freedom and the Freudian "death drive," which is

also a drive to sabotage one's inclination toward pleasure. And is this not why Freud was so fascinated by Michelangelo's *Moses*? He read the statue as depicting the moment when, full of rage and intending to smash the tablets containing the Decalogue, Moses summons up the strength to stop his act in the midst of its execution.... The implication is precisely that we ... obey an order which goes against our spontaneous inclination. Here, Badiou is wrong: the elementary ethical gesture is a negative one, the one of blocking one's direct inclination.[34]

The kind of freedom experienced in such a negative ordeal is presented by Freud as the highest accomplishment of the ethical will. It opens a possibility in the very absence of future.

V. PLASTICITY AND AUTOBIOGRAPHY

Existence is not a transparent and inoffensive grammatical or logical category, a harmless property of persons, animals, and things. Existence reveals itself as plasticity, as the very material of presence, as marble is the material of sculpture. It is capable of receiving any kind of form, but it also has the power to give form to itself. Being the stuff of things, it has the power both to shape and to dissolve a particular facet of individuality. A lifetime always proceeds within the boundaries of a double excess: an excess of reification and an excess of fluidification. When identity tends toward reification, the congealing of form, one can become the victim of highly rigid frameworks whose temporal solidification produces the appearance of unmalleable substance. Plasticity situates itself in the middle of these two excesses.

The decision to write *Plasticity at the Dusk of Writing* in the first person, the decision to say "I" and to speak of my own intellectual itinerary, is not a presumptuous or narcissistic claim. I know perfectly well that people won't be interested in "me." The book must be read as a narrative, written by a fictitious subject, whose reality is of no importance. I am just trying to show how a being, in its fragile and finite mutability, can experience the materiality of existence and transform its ontological meaning. The impossibility of fleeing means first of all the impossibility of fleeing oneself. It is within the very frame of this impossibility that I propose a philosophical change of perspective that focuses on closure as its principal object. Neural organization reveals the constant richness of possibilities that animates the finite and auto-organized nervous system. *The Brain That Changes Itself*:[35] this recent book's title expresses metaphorically, according to me, via neural plasticity, the very situation of the philosopher today. A brain that changes itself. That is exactly what "I" am.

Paris, December 2008

Notes

FOREWORD

1. Catherine Malabou, *The Future of Hegel: Plasticity, Temporality, and Dialectic*, trans. Lisabeth Durling (London: Routledge, 2005), 112.
2. Malabou, *The Future of Hegel*, 113. See also Cyril O'Regan, *The Heterodox Hegel* (Albany: State University of New York Press, 1994).
3. Malabou, *The Future of Hegel*, 119.
4. Catherine Malabou and Jacques Derrida, *Counter-Path: Traveling with Jacques Derrida*, trans. David Wills (Stanford, Calif.: Stanford University Press, 2004), 10.
5. Malabou and Derrida, *Counter-Path*, 285.
6. See Catherine Malabou, *What Should We Do with Our Brain?*, trans. Marc Jeannerod (New York: Fordham University Press, 2008), 5.
7. Malabou, *What Should We Do with Our Brain?*, 4.
8. Malabou, *What Should We Do with Our Brain?*, 80.
9. Catherine Malabou, *Les Nouveaux Blessés: De Freud à la neurologie, penser les traumatismes contemporains* (Paris: Bayard, 2007), 151–152.
10. Malabou, *Les Nouveaux Blessés*, 342.
11. See Martin Hagglund, *Radical Atheism: Derrida and the Time of Life* (Stanford, Calif.: Stanford University Press, 2008), which argues that Derrida insists upon

FOREWORD

a finite, immanent survivability rather than a pure ethical infinity of justice, as in Levinas.

12. This section is derived in part from a co-authored article by myself and Catherine Malabou, "Plasticity and the Future of Philosophy and Theology," published in a special issue (edited by Creston Davis) of the journal *Political Theology* in 2009. All of the text that appears here in this introduction is my own, although I want to acknowledge and thank Catherine Malabou for co-writing the original article and for clarifying specific queries I had about her work and thought. In addition, I gave a presentation based on this work at the American Academy of Religion annual meeting in Chicago, November 2008, as part of a panel session responding to Jean-Luc Nancy's idea of the deconstruction of Christianity.

13. See Marcel Gauchet, *The Disenchantment of the World: A Political History of Religion*, trans. Oscar Burge (Princeton, N.J.: Princeton University Press, 1997).

14. Jacques Derrida, *Specters of Marx: The State of the Debt, The Work of Mourning, and the New International*, trans. Peggy Kamuf (London: Routledge, 1994), 59.

15. Derrida, *Specters of Marx*, 59.

16. Derrida, *Specters of Marx*, 167.

17. See Tomoko Masuzawa, *The Invention of World Religions* (Chicago: University of Chicago Press, 2005), 145.

18. Masuzawa, *The Invention of World Religions*, 301.

19. Mohammed Arkoun, *Islam: To Reform or to Subvert?* (London: Saqi Books, 2006), 13.

20. Jean-Luc Nancy, *Dis-Enclosure: The Deconstruction of Christianity*, trans. Bettina Bergo, Gabriel Malenfant, and Michael B. Smith (New York: Fordham University Press, 2008), 140. This essay was originally published in English as Jean-Luc Nancy, "The Deconstruction of Christianity," in *Religion and Media*, ed. Hent de Vries and Samuel Weber (Stanford, Calif.: Stanford University Press, 2001), 112–130.

21. Nancy, *Dis-Enclosure*, 141.

22. Nancy, *Dis-Enclosure*, 145.

23. Jacques Derrida, *On Touching—Jean-Luc Nancy*, trans. Christine Irizarry (Stanford, Calif.: Stanford University Press, 2005), 54.

24. See Derrida, *On Touching—Jean-Luc Nancy*, 60: "Let us never forget that Christian, in fact, Lutheran, memory of Heideggerian deconstruction (*Destruktion* was first *destructio* by Luther, anxious to reactivate the originary sense of the Gospels by deconstructing theological sediments)."
25. See Martin Heidegger, *The Phenomenology of Religious Life*, trans. Matthias Fritsch and Jennifer Anna Gosetti-Ferencei (Bloomington: Indiana University Press, 2004).
26. Derrida, *On Touching—Jean-Luc Nancy*, 60.
27. Jacques Derrida, *Of Grammatology*, trans. Gayatri Chakravorty Spivak (Baltimore, Md.: The Johns Hopkins University Press, 1976), 68.
28. Gilles Deleuze, *Cinema 2: The Time-Image*, trans. Hugh Tomlinson and Robert Galeta (Minneapolis: University of Minnesota Press, 1989), 17.
29. Malabou, *What Should We Do with Our Brain?*, 39.
30. Malabou, *What Should We Do with Our Brain?*, 38–39.
31. Nancy, *Dis-Enclosure*, 160.
32. Nancy, *Dis-Enclosure*, 160.
33. Margaret Atwood, *Surfacing* (New York: Random House, 1998 [1972]), 160.
34. Nancy, *Dis-Enclosure*, 160.
35. Nancy, *Dis-Enclosure*, 160.
36. Nancy, *Dis-Enclosure*, 161.
37. See my forthcoming book on *Radical Political Theology* to be published by Columbia University Press.
38. Jacques Derrida, "Faith and Knowledge: The Two Sources of 'Religion' at the Limit of Reason Alone," in *Religion*, ed. Jacques Derrida and Gianni Vattimo (Stanford, Calif.: Stanford University Press, 1998), 51.
39. Nancy, *Dis-Enclosure*, 160.

TRANSLATOR'S INTRODUCTION

1. Catherine Malabou, *La Plasticité au soir de l'écriture: Dialectique, destruction, déconstruction* (Paris: Éditions Léo Scheer, 2005), 7.
2. Malabou, *La Plasticité au soir de l'écriture*, 7.

3. Catherine Malabou, *What Should We Do with Our Brain?*, trans. Marc Jeannerod (New York: Fordham University Press, 2008), 11.

PLASTICITY AT THE DUSK OF WRITING

1. I shall refer to books I have published, which include *L'Avenir de Hegel. Plasticité, temporalité, dialectique* (Paris: Vrin, 1996); *The Future of Hegel: Plasticity, Temporality and Dialectic,* trans. Lisabeth During (New York: Routledge, 2005); with Jacques Derrida: *The Contre-allée* (Paris: La Quinzaine Littéraire—Louis Vuitton, 1999); *Counterpath: Traveling with Jacques Derrida,* trans. David Wills (Stanford, Calif.: Stanford University Press, 2004); *Plasticité,* actes du colloque du Fresnoy (Paris: Editions Léo Scheer, 2000); *Le Change Heidegger. Du fantastique en philosophie* (Paris: Editions Léo Scheer, 2004); and *Que faire de notre cerveau?* (Paris: Bayard, 2004); *What Should We Do with Our Brain?*, trans. Sebastian Rand (New York: Fordham University Press, 2008).
2. Claude Lévi-Strauss, *The Way of the Masks,* trans. S. Modelsi (Seattle: University of Washington Press, 1982), 5. One room in the American Museum of Natural History in New York is devoted entirely to Native American art from the northwestern coast of the United States and Canada. Some of the most beautiful transformational masks in the world are to be found here. This is how Lévi-Strauss described the room: "There is in New York . . . a magical place where the dreams of childhood hold a rendezvous, where century-old tree trunks sing and speak, where indefinable objects watch out for the visitor, with the anxious stare of human faces, where animals of superhuman gentleness join their little paws like hands in prayer for the privilege of building the palace of the beaver for the chosen one, of guiding him to the realm of the seals, or of teaching him, with a mystic kiss, the language of the frog or the kingfisher. This place, on which outmoded but singularly effective museographic methods have conferred the additional allurements of the chiaroscuro of caves and the tottering heap of lost treasures, may be seen daily from ten to five o'clock at the American Museum of Natural History. It is the vast ground-floor gallery devoted to the Indians of the Pacific Northwest Coast, an area extending from Alaska to British Columbia." Lévi-Strauss, *The Way of the Masks,* 3.
3. Lévi-Strauss, *The Way of the Masks,* 8.

4. "Split representation" is analyzed in detail in chapter 13, "Split Representation in the Art of Asia and America," in Claude Lévi-Strauss, *Structural Anthropology*, vol. 1, trans. Claire Jacobson and Brooke Grundfest Schoepf (New York: Basic Books, 1963).
5. Lévi-Strauss, *Structural Anthropology*, 1:260.
6. Lévi-Strauss, *Structural Anthropology*, 1:261.
7. Jacques Derrida, *Of Grammatology*, trans. Gayatri Chakravorty Spivak (Baltimore, Md.: The Johns Hopkins University Press, 1974), 24.
8. On this point, see my article "Une différence d'écart: Heidegger et Lévi-Strauss," *La Revue Philosophique* 4 (October–December 2002): 403–416.
9. Malabou, *The Future of Hegel*, 13.
10. Malabou, *Le Change Heidegger*, 97.
11. I coined the term "schizology" to describe a contradiction that does not have a dialectical solution. It is well known that the great readers of Hegel—Heidegger, Kojève, Koyré, Hyppolite—see a hidden contradiction at work even in Hegel's own texts and that they claim thereby to detect a "schizological" pathology of the dialectic. See my article "Négatifs de la dialectique. Entre Hegel et le Hegel de Heidegger: Hyppolite, Koyré, Kojève," in *Philosophie* 52, *Hegel: Etudes* (Paris: Editions of Minuit, 1996), 37–53.
12. Lévi-Strauss, *The Way of the Masks*, 8.
13. A reminder that the etymology of the word "plasticity"—the Greek *plassein*, to model, to mold—points to two principal meanings. It refers both to the aptitude to *receive form* (for instance, clay is "plastic") and the ability to *give form* (as in the plastic arts or plastic surgery), but it is also characterized by the power to annihilate form. Let us not forget that the "plastic explosive" related to "bombing" "is an explosive substance made of nitroglycerine and nitrocellulose capable of setting off violent detonations" [Translator's note: in French *le plastic* is more evidently derived from the two terms *plastiquage* and *plastiquer*]. Thus plasticity is clearly placed between two polar extremes, with the sensible figure that is the taking shape in form (sculpture or plastic objects) on the one side and the destruction of all form (explosion) on the other.
14. G. W. F. Hegel, *The Phenomenology of Spirit*, trans. A. V. Miller (Oxford: Oxford University Press, 1977), cited in Malabou, *The Future of Hegel*, 11.

15. Malabou, *The Future of Hegel*, 187.
16. Martin Heidegger, "Art and Space," *Man and World* 6, no. 1 (1973): 3–8, 5.
17. Heidegger, "Art and Space," 8.
18. Heidegger, "Art and Space," 3.
19. Heidegger, "Art and Space," 5.
20. Derrida, *Of Grammatology*, 24.
21. Malabou, *Plasticité*.
22. Derrida, *Of Grammatology*, 55.
23. Derrida, *Of Grammatology*, 56.
24. The concept of motor scheme is taken also partly from Bergson. Bergson defines a motor scheme as the physical coordination that prepares and precedes movement, the preinscription of action in the body, a set of kinesthetic sensations.
25. "Helpline": Heidegger's expression is found in *Parmenides*, G. A., Bd 54, 80, at the moment when the philosopher defines the phrase *Wandel der Wahrheit*, "change of truth." See *Le Change Heidegger*, 92.
26. Hegel, *Phenomenology of Spirit*, 143, cited in Malabou, *The Future of Hegel*, 18.
27. Michel Serres, *Hermès I. La Communication* (Paris: Editions of Minuit, 1968), 25; my translation.
28. Serres, *Hermès*, 23; my translation.
29. Freud, *Mourning and Melancholia* [1919], in *The Standard Edition of the Complete Psychological Works of Sigmund Freud*, trans. James Strachey (London: Hogarth Press, 1981 [1919]), 17:57.
30. Jacques Derrida, *Specters of Marx*, trans. Peggy Kamuf (New York: Routledge, 1994), 36.
31. Claude Lévi-Strauss, *Tristes Tropiques*, trans. John Russell (New York: Athenaeum, 1968), 77–78.
32. Heidegger, Martin. "Language in the Poem," in *On the Way to Language*, trans. Peter D. Hertz (New York: Harper & Row Publishers, 1971). "From another sense and another image, evening transmutes . . . thinking [*verwandelt aus anderem Bild und anderem Sinn . . . das Denken*]" (172).
33. In the preface to this work, Hegel specifies that "the science of logic . . . constitutes metaphysics proper or purely speculative philosophy." *Hegel's Science of Logic*, I,

The Doctrine of Being, trans. A. V. Miller (Atlantic Highlands, N.J.: Humanities Press, 1969), 27.

34. For a presentation of dual temporality, see Malabou, *The Future of Hegel*, 201ff.
35. Martin Heidegger, *Being and Time*, trans. Joan Stambaugh (Albany: State University of New York Press, 1996), 20.
36. Heidegger, *Being and Time*, 20.
37. Martin Heidegger, *What Is Philosophy?*, trans. William Kluback and Jean T. White (Woodbridge, Conn.: Twayne Publishers Inc., 1958), 71.
38. Jacques Derrida, "Letter to a Japanese Friend," in *Derrida and Différence*, ed. David Wood and Robert Bernasconi (Evanston, Ill.: Northwestern University Press, 1988), 1.
39. Derrida, "Letter to a Japanese Friend," 3.
40. Derrida, "Letter to a Japanese Friend," 4.
41. Jacques Derrida, *Mémoires, pour Paul de Man* (Paris: Galilée, 1988), 38.
42. Martin Heidegger, *Hegel's Phenomenology of Spirit*, trans. Parvis Emad and Kenneth Maly (Bloomington: Indiana University Press, 1988).
43. Martin Heidegger, *Hegel, G. A.*, Bd 68. The volume is composed of two studies: (1) *Die Negativität. Eine Auseinandersetzung mit Hegel aus dem Ansatz in der Negativität*, and (2) *Erläuterung der "Einleitung" zu Hegels "Phänomenologie des Geistes."* This volume has not been translated into English, although it does exist in a French translation.
44. Martin Heidegger, *Identity and Difference*, trans. Joan Stambaugh (New York: Harper & Row, 1969).
45. Martin Heidegger, "Hegel's Concept of Experience," in *Heidegger: Off the Beaten Track*, trans. Julian Young and Kenneth Haynes (Cambridge: Cambridge University Press, 2002), 86–156.
46. According to Heidegger, as he demonstrates in the penultimate paragraph of *Being and Time*, this formal concept of the negative, or "abstract negativity," is fulfilled in Hegelian thought on temporality.
47. Martin Heidegger, "Hegel's Concept of Experience," 174.
48. Martin Heidegger, *Contributions to Philosophy (From Enowning)*, trans. Parvis Emad and Kenneth Maly (Bloomington: Indiana University Press, 2000).

49. See the passage on the difference between *aufheben*, to sublate dialectically, and *einspringen*, to substitute spontaneously, in Malabou, *Le Change Heidegger*, 139–145.
50. Malabou, *The Future of Hegel*, 9.
51. Malabou, *The Future of Hegel*, 13.
52. Malabou, *The Future of Hegel*, 13.
53. Malabou, *The Future of Hegel*, 134.
54. Malabou, *The Future of Hegel*, 155.
55. Martin Heidegger, *Hegel's Phenomenology of Spirit*, trans. P. Emad and K. Maly (Bloomington: Indiana Press, 1988), 147, cited with a modified translation in Malabou, *The Future of Hegel*, 4.
56. Heidegger, *Hegel*, my translation. In particular see section 5 of *Die Negativität* . . . : "*Negativität und Anderssein.*"
57. Heidegger, *Hegel*, 18, my translation.
58. Heidegger, "Being as Immutability," 16, my translation.
59. Heidegger goes so far as to claim that *Erfahrung* or "experience" could be translated by *metabolè. Erläuterung*, 106.
60. Martin Heidegger, "On the Essence and Concept of Φύσις in Aristotle's *Physics* B, I," in *Pathmarks*, trans. William McNeill (Cambridge: Cambridge University Press, 1998), 183–230, 190.
61. Heidegger, *Die Negativität* . . . , *Hegel*, 17–18, my translation.
62. Heidegger, *Die Negativität* . . . , *Hegel*, 53–54, my translation.
63. Malabou, *The Future of Hegel*, 192.
64. "Only a God Can Save Us: *Der Spiegel*'s Interview with Martin Heidegger" (1966), in *The Heidegger Controversy: A Critical Reader*, trans. Richard Wollin (Cambridge: The MIT Press, 1991), 91–116, 107.
65. On this point, see the general conclusion of Malabou, *Le Change Heidegger*.
66. As I tried to show in chapter 3 of the first part of *Le Change Heidegger*, devoted to Nietzsche.
67. Martin Heidegger, *Nietzsche*, trans. Joan Stambaugh, David Farrell Krell, and Frank A. Capuzzi (San Francisco: Harper & Row, 1987), 3:29, cited in Malabou, *Le Change Heidegger*, 111.
68. On "the poetizing essence of reason [*das dichtdende Wesent der Vernunft*]," see also Heidegger, *Nietzsche*, 3:94ff.

69. This is especially evident when Heidegger rolls out what I called, following Proust, the "moving walkways" of metaphysics. Malabou, *Le Change Heidegger*, 67.
70. I develop an initial analysis of the fantastic in philosophy in "*Pierre aime les horranges*, Une approche du fantastique en philosophie," in *Sens en tous sens. Autour du travail de Jean-Luc Nancy* (Paris: Galilée, 2004).
71. Malabou, *The Future of Hegel*, 156.
72. Malabou, *The Future of Hegel*, 126.
73. For Hegel, figuration is the work of imaging in art. It is the representation at work in the temporal sequencing typical of religion. As the third moment of absolute spirit, philosophy sublates them both.
74. The metamorphosized person founds and houses the truth of being (*Seyn*) "through the transformation of being in being itself." Martin Heidegger, *Basic Questions of Philosophy: Selected "Problems" of "Logic,"* trans. Richard Rojcewicz and André Schuwer (Bloomington: Indiana University Press, 1994).
75. For a definition of cineplastic, a term borrowed from Elie Faure, see Malabou, *Le Change Heidegger*, 132.
76. I also seek to develop this question of transformation as the effect of a double mode of being in my work on Judith Butler and more generally on queer theory.
77. Martin Heidegger, "Hebel—Friend of the House," in *Contemporary German Philosophy*, trans. Bruce V. Flotz and Michael Heim (1983), 3:92.
78. Martin Heidegger, "Für René Char" (1963), in *Denkerfahrungen*, 115.
79. Emmanuel Levinas, *Time and the Other*, trans. Richard A. Cohen (Pittsburgh, Penn.: Duquesne University Press, 1987), 45–46.
80. Levinas, *Time and the Other*, 46–47.
81. Emmanuel Levinas, *Existence and Existents*, trans. Alphonso Lingis (Dordrecht: Kluwer Academic Publishers, 1978), 59.
82. Levinas, *Existence and Existents*, 59.
83. Emmanuel Levinas, *Totality and Infinity: An Essay on Exteriority*, trans. Alphonso Lingis (Pittsburgh, Penn.: Duquesne University Press, 1969), 46.
84. Emmanuel Levinas, *Otherwise Than Being or Beyond Essence*, trans. Alphonso Lingis (Dordrecht: Kluwer Academic Publishers, 1991), 3.
85. Levinas, *Otherwise Than Being*, 3.
86. Heidegger, *On the Way to Language*, 57.

87. Heidegger, *On the Way to Language*, 48.
88. Heidegger, "Wenn *jener Gedanke über dich Gewalt bekäme, er würde dich, wie du bist, verwandeln und vielleicht zermalmen*," in Heidegger, *Nietzsche*, 2:20, translation modified.
89. Heidegger, *Nietzsche*, 1:149.
90. Heidegger, *Nietzsche*, 1:149.
91. Jean-Paul Sartre, *Aminadab: Or the Fantastic Considered as a Language*, trans. Annette Michelson (New York: Criterion Books, 1955), 67. Sartre also says: "The fantastic is the revolt of means against ends; either the object in question noisily asserts itself as a means, concealing its end through the very violence of its assertion, or it refers back to another means, and this one to still another, and so on *ad infinitum*, without our ever being able to discover the ultimate end, or else some interference in means belonging to independent series gives us a glimpse of a composite and blurred image of contradictory ends" (61).
92. See Heidegger's reading "The Turning," in which he claims: "When insight comes disclosingly to pass, then men are the ones who are struck in their essence by the flashing of Being. In insight, men are the ones who are caught sight of. Only when man, in the disclosing coming-to-pass of the insight by which he himself is beheld, renounces human self-will and projects himself toward that insight, away from himself, does he correspond in his essence to the claim of that insight." In *The Question Concerning Technology and Other Essays*, trans. William Lovitt (New York: Harper, 1977), 47.
93. On this point, see Jacques Derrida's analysis in *Of Sprit: Heidegger and the Question*, trans. Geoffrey Bennington and Rachel Bowlby (Chicago: University of Chicago Press, 1989).
94. Since Marx we know that the question of value is inseparable from phantasmagoria or the logic of phantasm.
95. Heidegger, *Basic Questions of Philosophy*.
96. Levinas, *Otherwise Than Being*, 90.
97. In his reading of Levinas developed in *Violence and Metaphysics*, Derrida declares: "if one does not follow Levinas when he affirms that the true resistance to the same is not that of things, is not *real*, but rather is *intelligible*, and if one rebels against the notion of a purely intelligible resistance, then in all these cases one will

follow Levinas no further." *Writing and Difference,* trans. Alan Bass (Chicago: University of Chicago Press, 1978), 94.
98. Levinas, *Otherwise Than Being,* 90.
99. Levinas, *Totality and Infinity,* 66.
100. Levinas, *Totality and Infinity,* 198.
101. Levinas, *Otherwise Than Being,* 90.
102. Levinas, *Totality and Infinity,* 50–51.
103. Levinas, *Totality and Infinity,* 65–66.
104. Jacques Derrida, "*Différance,*" in *Margins of Philosophy,* trans. Alan Bass (Chicago: University of Chicago Press, 1982), 7–8.
105. Derrida, "*Différance,*" 8.
106. Derrida, "*Différance,*" 10.
107. Derrida, "Form and Meaning," in *Margins of Philosophy,* 157–158.
108. Derrida, "*Différance,*" 22–23.
109. "Différance," he continues, "is not exactly a form, because it "can never be presented." Derrida, "*Différance,*" 23.
110. Emmanuel Levinas, *Humanism of the Other,* trans. Nidra Poller (Urbana: University of Illinois Press, 2003).
111. Levinas, *Humanism of the Other,* 62: "One stone scored another . . ."
112. Jacques Derrida, *Dissemination* (Chicago: University of Chicago Press, 1981), 32.
113. Derrida, "White Mythology," in *Margins of Philosophy,* 215.
114. On this point, see in particular Martin Heidegger, *What Is a Thing?,* trans. W. B. Barton Jr. and Vera Deutsch. (Lanham, Md.: University Press of America, 1985).
115. Giuseppe Penone, "*Répéter la forêt,*" in *Respirer l'ombre* (Paris: École nationale supérieure des beaux-arts, 1999), 58. With the series *Arbres* [Trees] and *Répéter la forêt* [Repeat the forest], Penone established a principle of the self-formation of the work. The sculptor does not create. Instead, he causes the form to appear by removing the tree's growth rings until he finds its heart: the tree, as a prefiguration of itself, thereby comes to light.
116. See Malabou, *Le Change Heidegger,* 232.
117. Martin Heidegger, *Kant and the Problem of Metaphysics,* trans. Richard Taft (Bloomington: Indiana University Press, 1990).
118. Derrida, *Dissemination,* 4.

119. The term "imaginal" describes an undifferentiated structure of the larvae of insects, which is destined to become an organ determined in the adult (cf. imago). *Cellules imaginales; disques imaginaux.*

120. Philippe Lacoue-Labarthe, "Typologies," in *Mimesis des articulations* (Paris: Aubier-Flammarion, 1975); *La Fiction du politique* (Paris: Bourgois, 1987), 103; *Heidegger, La politique du poème* (Paris: Galilée, 2002), 32, *passim*. On this issue, see my article "L'insistance de la forme. A propos du livre of Philippe Lacoue-Labarthe, *The Politique du poème*," *Poésie* 105 (October 2003): 154–159.

121. Claude Lanzmann, *Au sujet de Shoah, le film of Claude Lanzmann* (Paris: Belin, 1990), 301.

122. Jean-François Lyotard, *Discours, Figure*, 4th ed. (Paris: Klincksieck, 1985), 83.

123. Lyotard, *Discours, Figure*, 129.

124. Jean-François Lyotard, "Taking the Side of the Figural," in *The Lyotard Reader and Guide*, ed. K. Crome and J. Williams (New York: Columbia University Press, 2006), 38.

125. Lyotard, "Taking the Side of the Figural," 37.

126. Lyotard, "Taking the Side of the Figural," 37.

127. Lyotard, "Taking the Side of the Figural," 39.

128. For a new definition of the figure, see also Gilles Deleuze, *Francis Bacon, La logique de la sensation* (Paris: Seuil, 2002), especially 59ff.

129. François Jacob, *The Logic of Life*, trans. Betty E. Spillmann (Princeton, N.J.: Princeton University Press, 1973), 251.

130. Derrida, *Of Grammatology*, 9.

131. Jean-Pierre Changeux, *Neuronal Man: The Biology of Mind*, trans. Laurence Garey (New York: Pantheon Books, 1985), xiii.

132. Jean-Pierre Changeux and Paul Ricœur, *What Makes Us Think? A Neuroscientist and a Philosopher Argue About Ethics, Human Nature, and the Brain*, trans. M. B. DeBevoise (Princeton, N.J.: Princeton University Press, 2000), 152.

133. Changeux and Ricœur, *What Makes Us Think?*, 171.

134. On this point, see Changeux, *Neuronal Man*, 80.

135. Changeux, *Neuronal Man*, 168.

136. Changeux, *Neuronal Man*, 169.

137. Lévi-Strauss, *The Way of the Masks*, 10–12.

AFTERWORD

1. Sigmund Freud, *Instincts and Their Vicissitudes*, in *The Standard Edition of the Complete Psychological Works of Sigmund Freud*, ed. James Strachey (London: Norton, 1961), vol. 14.
2. Sigmund Freud, *Repression*, SE, vol. 14.
3. Emmanuel Levinas, *Totality and Infinity*, trans. Alphonso Lingis (Pittsburgh, Penn.: Duquesne University Press, 2005 [1961]), 33.
4. Martin Heidegger, *Being and Time*, trans. Joan Stambaugh (Albany: State University of New York Press, 1996), §13, 58 [62].
5. Heidegger, *Being and Time*, §39, 169 [181].
6. Heidegger, *Being and Time*, §69, 322 [351].
7. Heidegger, *Being and Time*, §38, 164 [176].
8. Heidegger, *Being and Time*, §38, 167 [179].
9. Heidegger, *Being and Time*, §38, 167 [179].
10. Heidegger, *Being and Time*, §7, 32 [36].
11. Heidegger, *Being and Time*, §60, 274 [298]
12. Jean-Luc Nancy, "The Decision of Existence," in *The Birth to Presence*, trans. Brian Holmes (Stanford, Calif.: Stanford University Press), 1993.
13. Nancy, "The Decision of Existence," 82.
14. Translated freely from Maurice Blanchot, *De Kafka à Kafka* (Paris: Gallimard, "Folio Essai," 1981), 73.
15. Jacques Derrida, *Adieu to Emmanuel Levinas*, trans. Pascal-Anne Brault and Michel Naas (Stanford, Calif.: Stanford University Press, 1999), 55.
16. Derrida, *Adieu to Emmanuel Levinas*, 55.
17. Derrida, *Adieu to Emmanuel Levinas*, 56.
18. Derrida, *Adieu to Emmanuel Levinas*, 41.
19. Jacques Derrida, "Point de folie—Maintenant l'architecture" (1986), reprinted in *Architecture Theory Since 1968*, ed. K. Michael Hays (Cambridge, Mass.: MIT Press, 1998), 566–581, 570.
20. Levinas, *Totality and Infinity*, 192.
21. Roland Barthes, "Plastic," in *Mythologies*, trans. Annette Lavers (New York: Hill and Wang, 1972), 97.

22. Jacques Derrida, "A Time for Farewells: Heidegger (read by) Hegel (read by) Malabou," foreword to Catherine Malabou, *The Future of Hegel: Plasticity, Temporality, and Dialectic* (New York: Routledge, 2005), 32.
23. Jacques Derrida, "Faith and Knowledge," in *Acts of Religion* (New York: Routledge, 2002), 56.
24. Derrida, "A Time for Farewells," 32.
25. Derrida, "A Time for Farewells," 32–33.
26. Derrida, "A Time for Farewells," 34.
27. Derrida, "A Time for Farewells," 47.
28. Jacques Derrida, *Margins Of Philosophy*, trans. Alan Bass (Chicago: University of Chicago Press, 1982), 25.
29. Catherine Malabou, *What Should We Do with Our Brain?*, trans. Sebastian Rand (New York: Fordham University Press, 2008).
30. Jacques Derrida, *Of Grammatology*, trans. Gayatri Chakravorty Spivak (Baltimore, Md.: Johns Hopkins University Press, 1976), 27.
31. Freud, *The Moses of Michelangelo*, SE, 13:229.
32. Freud, *The Moses of Michelangelo*, 13:229.
33. Freud, *The Moses of Michelangelo*, 13:233.
34. Slavoj Žižek, *The Parallax View* (Cambridge, Mass.: MIT Press, 2006), 202.
35. Norman Doidge, *The Brain That Changes Itself: Stories for Personal Triumph from the Frontiers of Brain Science* (London: Penguin Books, 2007).

Lightning Source UK Ltd.
Milton Keynes UK
UKHW011807170622
404595UK00002B/76